THE 30-DAY MONEY CLEANSE

TAKE CONTROL OF YOUR FINANCES,
MANAGE YOUR SPENDING, AND
DE-STRESS YOUR MONEY FOR GOOD

ASHLEY FEINSTEIN GERSTLEY

sourcebooks

Published by Sourcebooks, Inc.

P.O. Box 4410, Naperville, Illinois 60567-4410

(630) 961-3900

Fax: (630) 961-2168

sourcebooks.com

Library of Congress Cataloging-in-Publication data is on file with the publisher.

Printed and bound in the United States of America.

JOS 10 9 8 7 6 5 4

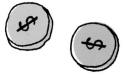

For anyone who has ever been
stressed about money.

CONTENTS

PREFACE
MY STORY

I BECAME AN EXPERT IN achieving financial freedom when I found myself constantly stressed over my money. Where was it always going? Despite being a finance major and a financial services professional, I knew absolutely nothing about my own money. And it seemed to me that if I was lost and overwhelmed, people without my background probably were too.

In almost every area of personal finance, I've learned lessons the hard way. There was the time I took a coworker's investment advice and lost thousands of dollars; the time I didn't realize that I needed to put my roommate's name on our renters' insurance policy, and then she wasn't able to use it when she really needed it; and the time I opened a store credit card that was so *not* user-friendly that my credit was blemished for seven years.

As I was going through my money journey, I experienced so much power and freedom from what I discovered about personal finance that I have since made it my mission to share the secret sauce with people everywhere. So many of us feel alone, confused, and worried that we're lagging behind where we think we "should" be when it comes to our money. But much of the material that's available on personal finance makes the topic unnecessarily daunting and boring—so we avoid it. I realized that what people needed was a simple, step-by-step plan that would help them take control of their money and get on track to reach their financial goals.

Thus, the 30-Day Money Cleanse was born. I designed the program based on my research and my work coaching clients one-on-one, which helped me see commonalities across all of my clients' financial frustrations and stressors. Our issues might manifest a bit differently, but we are all struggling with similar questions. I also realized that money is in many respects strikingly similar to food, especially in the way that our behaviors tend to be tied much more to our emotions than to facts and figures.

I initially created the 30-Day Money Cleanse three years ago as an online course, and the results since then have been tremendous. The average participant saves $950 over the thirty-day duration of the course, or more than 20 percent of their monthly pretax income. I knew from the success that participants were experiencing—and the positive feedback that I received from them—that I had to share the 30-Day Money Cleanse with an even wider audience. By writing this book, I aim to provide every reader with an easy-to-follow manual for achieving the healthy, lasting money mindset that this program has brought to me.

The 30-Day Money Cleanse is a movement to live an incredible, meaningful, and mindful life *now*, while also saving for our long-term goals and dreams. The Money Cleanse brings the "personal" back to "personal finance" and gets us back on our own team so that we can live in harmony with our money and build wealth easily.

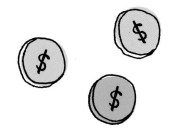

GETTING STARTED

CHAPTER ONE

WHY WE ALL NEED A
MONEY CLEANSE

> **"Our degree of resistance around money is proportional to the degree of power available to us on the other side of that resistance."**
>
> **—BARBARA STANNY, AUTHOR OF**
> *OVERCOMING UNDEREARNING*

I SPEND MOST OF MY day talking with people about what they view as one of the most secretive—and often shameful—parts of their lives: their money. They share their dreams, their fears, and the mistakes they've made, and I get a beautiful glimpse into their values, passions, upbringings, families, and goals. It's an absolute honor to join them on their money journey, because I get to travel with them from doubt, worry, and guilt to a stress-free and powerful money mindset. I feel like the luckiest woman on earth because I get to spend my days working on a mission that I'm truly passionate about.

Not only do I love talking about money with my clients, groups, and potential clients, but I also seem to attract money stories wherever I go. It might be a new friend sharing an anecdote over a glass of wine, a colleague chiming in about a personal experience on a business call, or a complete stranger telling me about the money drama in their family. I've listened to thousands and thousands of people share information about their secret money lives, and it didn't take a rocket scientist to notice that there were some major trends in all of their stories.

Regardless of how successful we are or how much money we make, we're all struggling with very similar issues when it comes to our money. And to make matters worse, we feel completely alone.

Here are some of the complaints I hear over and over:

$\text{\textcircled{\$}}$ "It's not like I'm only buying high-end products or going on tons of shopping sprees... I really don't live an extravagant lifestyle, but for some reason, there's never enough money left over to save."

$\text{\textcircled{\$}}$ "I thought I wasn't getting paid enough to save, but then I got a raise, and I'm still not saving. Where is all of my money going?!"

$\text{\textcircled{\$}}$ "I am so successful in every other area of my life. Why can't I figure out this money stuff? If I had a plan, I would be able to execute it. I just don't know where to start."

The first thing we have to understand about money is that we can't avoid it. We might think we're doing ourselves a favor by ignoring our ever-growing credit card bills or not looking at our bank accounts, but that actually ends up causing us more anxiety in the long run. As hard as we may try, we really can't avoid money altogether. We might be able to take a break for a day or two, but in order to live as functioning members of society, we have to deal with money.

Yet most of us didn't learn about money. The majority of high schools and colleges don't offer personal finance programs, and it's unlikely that a financially savvy adult or mentor took the time to fully delve into the topic with us. It's pretty funny when you think about it: personal finance is something that every single one of us will need, but it's not something that we're formally taught. We spend semesters learning calculus and geometry (and I don't know about you, but I haven't used either since), yet when it comes to something this practical, this necessary—not a single lesson.

To make matters worse, it's taboo to talk about money! Have you ever noticed that we talk to our friends about almost everything—from our deepest secrets to the most intimate details of our dating lives—but not about how much we earn? We might allude to our expensive rent or talk about a recent purchase we got on sale, but we don't talk about whether we're investing, saving for retirement, or trying (maybe unsuccessfully) to save money.

This taboo extends even to our most intimate relationships. Twenty-five percent of newlyweds don't know how much their partner earns,[1] and five percent of couples have bank accounts that their partner doesn't know about.[2] We're not talking about money even with those closest to us, and it's holding us back. In fact, it's a common saying that it's impolite to talk about politics, religion, and *money*. But by avoiding the topic, we are forced to deal with the complex beast that is money on our own, completely unarmed! We are truly not set up for success.

See where I'm going here? On top of these standard challenges we have in tackling our finances, money is also extremely emotionally charged. As I mentioned earlier, money and food are similar in many ways. The numbers are actually pretty simple. For food: calories in minus calories out equals gaining, losing, or maintaining weight. With money, it's the same equation: money in minus money out equals savings that we can set aside for our goals, living beyond our means, or staying stuck right where we are. Of course, if it were really that easy, there wouldn't be a multibillion dollar weight-loss industry!

Our relationships with both money and food can wreak havoc on us emotionally because they appear to be the keys to our happiness. Money in particular is a tool that we can use to get and experience what we want in life. That's a powerful dynamic! But that dynamic is also a source of pressure and stress, and in many cases, instead of making us happy, it's the thing that's holding us back from what we really want.

——— Can money buy happiness? ———

The short answer is yes, but to a limited extent. According to a study led by researchers at Princeton University, psychologist Daniel Kahneman and economist Alan B. Krueger, "The belief that high income is associated with good mood is widespread but mostly illusory. People with above-average income are relatively satisfied with their lives but are barely happier than others in moment-to-moment experience, tend to be more tense, and do not spend more time in particularly enjoyable activities."[3] In another study, Kahneman and colleague Angus Deaton found that there's a point of diminishing returns when it comes to income and happiness:

$88,000.[4]* Above that point, more income does not increase our happiness.

Why? According to Kahneman, "When people have a lot more money, they can buy a lot more pleasures, but there are some indications that when you have a lot of money, you will savor each pleasure less." After the $88,000 threshold, "further increases in income no longer improve individuals' ability to

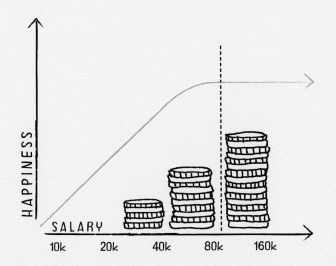

do what matters most to their emotional well-being, such as spending time with people they like, avoiding pain and disease, and enjoying leisure."

---

*   Figure is adjusted for inflation.

Technology has also completely changed our relationship with money, allowing us to more successfully disengage with it. Credit cards, online shopping, and subscriptions have removed from our lives the experience or pain of paying. We hop in and out of Ubers without taking out our wallets. We click one button on Amazon and boxes show up at our door. It's no wonder we have no idea where our money is going! And believe me, we really don't. Try guessing what you spent over the last month, week, or even day. You'd be shocked at some of the expenses that we forget about or rationalize away.

To top this off, we are also bombarded with people trying to sell us things all the time. Billion-dollar marketing budgets play off of our impulses and desires, show up in our internet searches, and make us think we need things that we otherwise wouldn't know existed. Think about the "treat yo'self" motto, for example. I'm all about giving ourselves what we deserve and knowing that we are worth it, but in many cases, we are treating ourselves at the expense of the things that we want most. If buying that new sweater or daily takeout keeps you from paying off your credit card debt or going on the vacation you've been dreaming about, is that really a treat?

Financial services offerings like credit cards and insurance products are no different. Companies play to our financial fears

The pain of paying: how to use it to our advantage.

Dan Ariely, professor of psychology and behavioral economics at Duke University, suggests that "the 'pain of paying' is magnified when our feelings about spending money are coupled with consumption."[5] That's why paying with cash typically feels worse than paying with credit cards. With credit cards, we pay later, which allows us to disassociate from the purchase.

As our pain of paying increases, we tend to spend less but also enjoy spending less, and vice versa. Here are ways you can either increase or decrease your pain of paying:

Increase pain of paying (decrease spending)	Decrease pain of paying (increase spending)
Use cash or debit card	Use credit cards
Receive notifications when money is spent	Keep payment hidden
Keep a money journal	Pay in advance
Pay for use (by the hour, or use of an item/service)	Sign up for unlimited use

and doubts, often making us feel stupid, in order to get us to purchase a product or service that we may or may not need. Not to mention that it might actually be harmful, not helpful, to our financial well-being. It's no wonder we aren't sure whom to trust or where to turn!

This anecdotal evidence is backed up by research and statistics. Money has been cited as the number one stressor for Americans by the American Psychological Association's (APA) *Stress in America* survey for ten out of the last eleven years (falling to the number two spot in 2017, after "the future of our nation").[6] This stress is not just affecting our emotional well-being. Stress impacts our core mindset, in addition to every physiological system in our bodies and our emotions. It even affects our productivity at work.

Here's a look at financial unwellness in America:

💲 The APA's 2017 *Stress in America* survey reports that 62 percent of Americans are stressed out about money.[7]

💲 According to a Federal Reserve Board survey, almost half of Americans (44 percent) couldn't cover a $400 emergency without borrowing money or selling something.[8] This statistic relates to adults in every age demographic.

- Thirty-four percent of Americans say they have $0 in savings—up from 28 percent in 2015—according to a 2016 GOBankingRates.com survey.[9] The same survey reports that the percentage of Americans with less than $1,000 in savings has jumped to 69 percent.

- The Economic Policy Institute reports that half of all Americans have nothing put away for retirement.[10]

- Debt and delinquency rates (a.k.a. not paying back your debt) are rising. The average household with student loan debt has accumulated $46,597 in student loans, and the average household carrying credit card debt has racked up $15,654 in credit card debt, according to a study conducted by NerdWallet.[11]

The good news is that, although the deck is stacked against us, we have the power to change the statistics and do something about our financial well-being. We can turn this entire paradigm right on its head and set ourselves up in a financially powerful way. That's where the Money Cleanse comes in. I'm going to help you do just that, step by step, by your side the entire time. Not only will we tackle the beast of money, but I can promise you, it will be fun too!

—— **Women have it worse.** ——

For women, things are even more dire. When you take into account the gender pay gap (women are earning $0.83, on average, for every $1.00 a man makes, according to the Pew Research Center, and the numbers are far worse for women of color[12]), the gender investing gap (meaning that women are investing a lot less than men and therefore not growing their money), and the fact that women are living much longer than men (and thus need more money to fund their retirement), women are starting at a major disadvantage. What's more, a "pink tax" on many products and services that are designed for or directly marketed to women, like clothing and hygiene products, means that women end up paying more than their male counterparts for the exact same or compa-rable items.[13] One or two dollars more for a basic T-shirt might not sound like much, but these types of purchases can add up to thousands of dollars extra that women are having to pay every year.

The first step is to get clear on why money is so difficult for us. When we see all of the logical things that might be holding us back in our money lives, we can understand why we are where we are. It makes sense why we're not flourishing! We can then muster up some compassion for ourselves and our current money situation. Compassion and understanding lead to forgiveness, which is the key to moving forward. Have you ever noticed how you talk to yourself about money? We punish ourselves, try to will ourselves into submission, and say terribly mean things, such as:

 "What's wrong with me? Why can't I figure this out?"

 "I'm an idiot."

"I'll always be terrible with money."

"I'll never be able to figure out my finances."

"I'm a failure."

"I'm worthless."

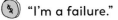 "I don't deserve financial freedom."

The list goes on and on… And guess what? It doesn't work!

To make progress in our money lives, it's necessary to get on our own team. The real trick is knowing that it doesn't have to be a battle, even though we're used to it feeling like one. What we want most is typically our number one goal, and achieving it would make us truly happy. We might *think* we want whatever instant purchase or impulse we yearn for in the moment, but we don't actually want that as much as we want our greater goal. Our financial lives can feel like never-ending confrontations with the devil on one shoulder and an angel on the other, but when you stop and think about it, you'll realize that you don't need to engage in this constant inner battle. You're on your own side.

I'm here to tell you that there is a ton of progress to be made in your money life, no matter what stage you're at, and it doesn't have to be hard. When you take this first step of compassion and forgiveness, the rest is easy. During your Money Cleanse, you will reconnect with your spending and notice what you say to yourself about money. You'll come back to the reasons discussed in this section about why we all need a Money Cleanse and remind yourself that it makes complete sense why you are where you are. It's called a journey for a reason; we are always improving and growing (and sometimes that means taking a step backward).

Through the Money Cleanse, you will learn a powerful new money language that will make the process of planning—and sticking to the plan—fun and enjoyable. You will experience many mindset shifts, and once you do, you won't look at money the same way again. It's a transformation. You will know how to achieve your goals, spend your money in meaningful ways aligned with your values, and let go of guilt and shame.

You will save money and be surprised that your lifestyle feels more meaningful and fulfilled at the same time. While many of the subjective benefits of the Money Cleanse are compelling, the quantifiable results are incredible as well. As I said, the average participant saves $950 while going through the program, or more than 20 percent of their pretax income. Multiply that by the months and years to come and that's a complete game changer for your goals.

You will also experience clarity and ease in other areas of your life as a result of the exercises and principles in this book, because they can be applied to anything. If your diet is feeling out of control, these same concepts can be applied to improve your relationship with food and nutrition. If you're trying to build a positive morning routine but it's not working, look at how you're talking to yourself about new habits. Are you clear on your **why**? It's all the same!

Let's begin!

CHAPTER TWO

HOW IT
WORKS

> **"The most effective way to do it is to do it."**
>
> **—AMELIA EARHART**

YOU ARE PROBABLY THINKING, *How is this possible? It sounds too good to be true that I could save so much more money while actually improving my lifestyle. Is this a trick? Where has the Money Cleanse been all my life?*

The good news is that this is the furthest thing from a trick.

One of the many reasons we all need a Money Cleanse is that we have become extremely disconnected from our spending. This is one of the first things we'll tackle in *The 30-Day Money Cleanse*. Throughout the book, we will go through exercises that make us increasingly conscious and aware of what we're spending. It sounds so simple, but just by seeing where our money is actually going, we take back a lot of power. **Magical things happen when we become aware.**

Why? We can see which expenses are adding value to our lives and which ones we're ready to let go of. We get clarity on how much we're spending per year on each expense, which can be a game changer for deciding how we want to continue spending going forward.

That's what awareness is all about. Facing the numbers can sound really scary, but it's almost always a huge relief to find out what's actually happening with our money. And it's often not as bad as we think. What might feel like our biggest problems can be fixed easily with a straightforward step or a group of steps.

Another reason the Money Cleanse works is that we experience tremendous mindset shifts. We move from a place of scarcity to one of abundance. What does a scarcity mindset look like? It's our default when it comes to money. When we're in a scarcity mindset, what we are earning will never be enough. There will always be more things and more experiences that we need or desire, so we'll always want to be earning more.

Most of us would absolutely love to double our salaries. Not only would we love it, but we'd also believe it would be the solution to all of our money problems. Think about it. Don't you? If your salary doubled, you'd be able to afford the things you want, you'd start saving meaningfully, or you'd finally get out of credit card debt. This is an illusion! According to a study conducted at Vanderbilt University, the bankruptcy rate among lottery winners is quadruple what it is for the general population.[14] Within three to five years after winning the lottery, too many people end up right back where they started, or even worse off—at zero.

Sports Illustrated reported in a 2009 study that after NFL players have been retired for two years, 78 percent go bankrupt or suffer from financial stress caused by joblessness or divorce.[15] Within five years of retirement, an estimated 60 percent of former NBA players are broke. As George S. Clason puts it in his book *The Richest Man in Babylon*, "What each of us calls our 'necessary expenses' will always grow to equal our incomes unless we protest to the contrary."[16] In other words, we can't just outearn our spending.

This is our scarcity mindset in action—and scarcity doesn't work. This mindset gets us back to the devil-and-angel-on-our-shoulders situation. We want things, but we deprive ourselves and try to punish ourselves into submission. We restrict ourselves, tell ourselves no, and then eventually rebel and derail ourselves. Not only does this not work for our goals, but it also deprives us of joy in our lives, because we get stuck in a cycle of making impulse buys, feeling terribly guilty, and then repeating the pattern all over again.

Moving to a mindset of abundance stops this cycle. It's a subtle shift, but people report that they just stopped craving, wanting, or needing things that they used to purchase. The serial shopper stops feeling the need to shop. The self-proclaimed coffee addict takes a different route to work and skips the coffee. Why does this happen?

When we come from a mindset of abundance, we already have more than enough. In the first week of the Money Cleanse, we'll work on letting go of all frivolous spending—however you choose to define it. When we strip out frivolous spending, we become aware of how much we already have. We'll take out many of the expenses in our day-to-day lives, but it won't feel that bad. It's a truly eye-opening exercise!

Letting go of our frivolous spending for a week also changes our habits. When we shed some of our regular expenses, we realize that we don't actually need them. In some cases, we might even be happier without them! This phenomenon is similar to a juice cleanse, in that it switches up our regular routine and helps us let go of some of our habits that don't serve us well.

You might notice that you have more energy when you bring your own healthy lunch to work instead of grabbing fast food midday, or that you don't mind the coffee at work and would rather put the money you'd typically spend at a coffee shop toward something more meaningful. Shaking up our routine allows us to step back and gain a new perspective. It can be a first step in letting go of an expense, or surprisingly, it can be all we need to do to make a change.

I've found that my most successful clients experience another very specific mindset shift during their money journey. They start to operate from a growth mindset, rather than a fixed mindset—a concept established by Carol Dweck, a professor of psychology at Stanford University and a leading researcher in the field of motivation. In her bestselling book *Mindset: The New Psychology of Success*, Dweck identifies two core mindsets:

1. A fixed mindset, the belief that one's abilities were predetermined at birth and are carved in stone.
2. A growth mindset, the belief that one's skills and qualities can be cultivated through effort and perseverance.[17]

These mindsets impact every area of our lives, from finance to education to equality to corporate culture (and beyond). In her 2014 TED talk, titled "The Power of Believing That You Can Improve," Dweck discusses an experiment that illuminates the difference between the two mindsets.[18] In the study, she gave ten-year-olds a problem that was slightly too hard for them. Those with a growth mindset said things like "I love a challenge" or "I was hoping this would be informative." These individuals wanted to learn and grow. Those with a fixed mindset, on the other hand, felt that it was tragic and catastrophic that they couldn't solve the puzzle easily. They felt that they had failed, which they equated with not being smart.

Long story short: Dweck's research shows that those with a fixed mindset run from difficulty, while those with a growth mindset engage with problems and puzzles and exhibit a willingness to learn and grow from challenges.

Think about your own mindset for a moment. How would you describe your behavior when you're confronted with difficulty and challenge?

....

....

....

....

....

....

....

....

....

....

....

....

....

You might notice that you are predominantly of the growth mindset, but that you can get triggered into a fixed mindset by certain topics, people, or situations. We all have our own triggers, and taking the time to understand them is one of the most important steps we can take in fostering a growth mindset.

For many of us, our finances in particular can trigger a fixed mindset. Even if we are confident in other areas of our lives—at work, in our relationships—we don't bring that same willingness to engage and learn to our personal finances. Our inabilities feel carved in stone, and it feels futile to even try to learn. So instead, we run away. This prevents us from facing what's happening in our financial life and keeps us from achieving our goals, which feels like yet another failure. A fixed mindset creates this endless cycle.

The work we do in the Money Cleanse helps us shift from a fixed to a growth mindset. First, we adjust our self-talk around setbacks and failure, approaching them from a place of nonjudgmental examination. It's all about the power of *yet*. You might not be where you want to be in your financial life *yet*, or this whole personal finance thing isn't working *yet*. With this shift, we're able to cultivate and grow our financial wellness, just like any other skill.

I can't start saving	...yet.
I don't know how to invest	...yet.
I'm not good at this whole money thing	...yet.
I don't get how I'll ever be able to pay off my student loans	...yet.
I don't know how I'll start saving for retirement	...yet.
This "being responsible with my money" thing doesn't work	...yet.

The Money Cleanse also illuminates our relationship with money. It might sound weird at first, but we have a relationship with money just like any other relationship in our lives. It's how we interact with and relate to money. Our relationship with money is created over time and can be influenced by many factors. We are guided by how our parents interacted with money. We're also shaped by mentors, teachers, friends, our experiences, and society as a whole.

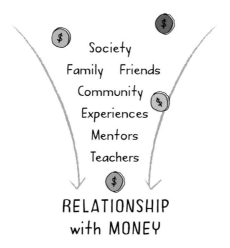

Society
Family   Friends
Community
Experiences
Mentors
Teachers

RELATIONSHIP
with MONEY

Try describing how you interact with and relate to money, and then translate those tendencies to an important personal relationship in your life. For example, how would things go with your best friends if you just ignored them? They probably wouldn't be too thrilled about it. The same goes for your money.

....
....
....
....
....

Even though our personal financial situation is extremely important to us, it's often one of the first areas of our lives that we neglect. This affects our results, how we reach our goals, and our well-being. What we pay attention to grows, so look out for positive signs in your money life.

As you become aware of your relationship with money, you might notice that you have some beliefs about money and yourself (or money in general) that can hold you back. For example, if someone was brought up thinking that money equates with greed, they're either going to have a very hard time earning money or a very hard time keeping that earned money in their bank account. And it makes complete sense! Why would anyone want to be greedy? If we truly believe that money means greed, we're not going to allow ourselves to acquire and keep it.

Beliefs that keep us from attracting and maintaining wealth:	Beliefs that help us attract and maintain wealth:
"Having money is greedy."	"I will do great things with my money."
"Money makes us evil."	"There is enough money for everyone."
"I hate money."	"I have everything I need and want."
"Money only comes from hard work and sacrifice."	"I am a money magnet."
"I don't deserve money."	"I am happy, healthy, and wealthy."
"Time is money."	"I am abundant."
"Rich people get there by taking advantage of others."	"Money makes me generous."

What are some of your beliefs about money?

There are people who experience success in their money goals by punishing themselves into submission (just like there are people who get great physical results through restrictive and punitive dieting regimes). But for most of us, this approach doesn't give us the results we're looking for, and it robs us of so much enjoyment and happiness in our lives. We can achieve our goals and have fun while doing so! It doesn't have to be one or the other.

When we become conscious and aware of what's happening with our money, we can foster that abundance mindset and create a harmonious relationship with money, which gives us the clarity and foundation to put together a plan. Until this wonderful trans-formation takes place, we won't be able to put together a powerful, meaningful plan.

For many people, the word *plan* suggests a terribly restrictive budget. But as we've seen, scarcity doesn't work. What we create during the Money Cleanse is far from a traditional budget. We create a "happiness allocation." A happiness allocation is a plan where we look at what money is coming in and decide how to allocate it in the ways that are going to make us the happiest in both the short- and long-term. No matter how much or how little we earn, at any given point in time, we have a certain amount of money (I call it our "pie"), and we only get to spend or use each

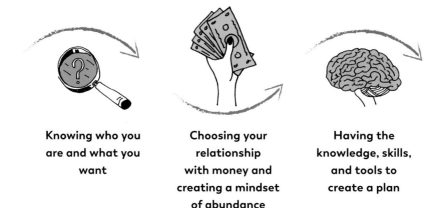

Knowing who you are and what you want

Choosing your relationship with money and creating a mindset of abundance

Having the knowledge, skills, and tools to create a plan

dollar that we have once. Why not work to maximize our true happiness per dollar?

Our happiness allocation eventually becomes our new money lifestyle. We are no longer Money Cleansing because we have created a new and powerful way to live that has us reaching our goals and maximizing the joy in our life based on our values.

This is why the program is actually easy. When you're enjoying life and spending your money in meaningful ways, it doesn't feel like you're missing out. Because you're coming from a place of forgiveness and compassion and have fostered a healthy relationship with money based on the idea of abundance, you realize that there is nothing you want more than your most coveted goals.

HAPPINESS ALLOCATION

Examples of Money Pies

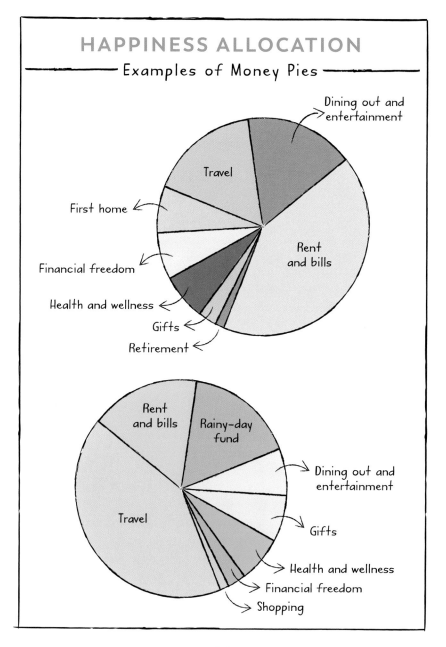

As you embark on your Money Cleanse, keep an open mind and participate fully in each of the exercises. Remember that each and every one of us can benefit from a Money Cleanse and that you are not alone in your journey. I'll walk you through each manageable step so that it's not overwhelming or daunting. If you expect tremendous results from yourself and the program, those results will materialize. If you are open to change and practice compassion and forgiveness along the way, I promise that you will get the results you are looking for.

CHAPTER THREE:

SETTING YOURSELF UP
FOR SuCCESS

> **"Do not wait until the conditions are perfect to begin. Beginning makes the conditions perfect."**
> **—ALAN COHEN**

WHEN IT COMES TO OUR money lives, and our lives in general, it's easy to get into the routine of *go, go, go!* We're part of a culture that rewards busyness and productivity. As a type A planner, I understand how amazing it feels to check something off of your to-do list. While accomplishing things feels great, and I wouldn't dare take that away from you during your Money Cleanse, it's important to take some time first to prepare for this journey and to reflect on it along the way.

It's tempting to jump right in, churn through the exercises, and then move on to the next thing, but I cannot overemphasize the value in taking the time to set yourself up for success and to truly reflect so that you can improve and adjust for the next week.

We also tend to want to wait until circumstances are perfect to get started on something big. You might want to wait until you have a month without many plans so you can stay home and cook yourself meals and do the program as "perfectly" and frugally as possible. Or if you travel a lot for work, your ideal month might be one in which you have very minimal travel plans. But if you're always waiting for the perfect conditions, you're never going to get started. What's more, a false reality that doesn't reflect what your life is usually like is actually the least helpful time to do the Money Cleanse.

The Money Cleanse is most valuable when it's integrated into your true daily life. If living your life includes work trips, time with friends, and celebrations, then these are all things that need to be part of your Money Cleanse. The things that you think will get in the way of doing the Money Cleanse are actually the things that will have the greatest impact on your money life. So if you have a busy week, a weekend full of fun plans, or an upcoming vacation, it's actually the perfect time to start your Money Cleanse!

That being said, you'll only get out of the Money Cleanse what you put into it, so it's important to create the time to read the chapters and do the exercises. I use the word *create* very intentionally. Despite what it often feels like, we are not at the mercy of our calendars—we actually have the power to decide what we spend our time on. Have you ever noticed that when you don't plan out your time, or don't put your to-do list in your calendar, things don't get done? This is Parkinson's Law at work.

Parkinson's Law is the idea that things take up as much space as we give them. Ever notice that your junk drawer always fills up, that meetings take up as much time as we allot them in the calendar, and that our spending always seems to reach the limit of our bank accounts (sometimes to the cent!)? That's Parkinson's Law doing its thing.

Parkinson's Law applies to every area of our lives. Once you know about it, you'll see it everywhere. When we first notice this phenomenon, it may be wreaking havoc on our lives, and that's okay. The good news is that once we know about it and recognize it, we can use it to help us reach our goals more quickly and easily.

Here are ways to use Parkinson's Law to your advantage in every area of your life:

Keep it simple. We can't do and have everything. Keep the big picture in mind and decide ruthlessly what you want to fill your time with and spend your money on.

Make goals with deadlines. Big, ambiguous goals are a Parkinson's Law trap. Have you ever had all day to do one thing, but it somehow doesn't get done? Me too! Break bigger goals down into small, specific steps, and set deadlines for each step.

Create time in the calendar. If you want to spend time on something, put it in your calendar (even if it's something small). Otherwise, your time will fill up, and you'll keep pushing it to a later date.

Give yourself less time to complete tasks. When you schedule time in your calendar, try giving yourself less time for each task. You might be surprised to find that you still manage to get everything done!

Set up tasks to be automatic whenever possible. When things are automated, they take no time at all, so you can rest assured that they will get done.

Use Parkinson's Law to your advantage by scheduling two hours in your calendar each week to dedicate to your Money Cleanse. This will give you enough time to read through the chapters and complete the exercises for each week. It doesn't have to be in two-hour chunks of time; you can decide how you want to include it in your calendar based on how you work best and what else is in your schedule.

If two hours doesn't seem manageable, given what you have going on in the next month, then you can decide intentionally to time your Money Cleanse differently. Also keep in mind that however you decide to set up your calendar now doesn't have to be set in stone. If you find two one-hour blocks per week to be difficult because you forget what you were working on in the first hour, or for some other reason, then you can always adjust.

Take a couple of minutes (if you haven't already) to think through how you want to space out your Money Cleanse. Then go and actually create weekly appointments in your calendar for each week of the program. You might have to rearrange your schedule a bit or let go of some commitments, but the time that you dedicate to your Money Cleanse will be worth it—I promise!

I know how difficult it can be to finish something that you start, but right here, in this moment, is when you'll understand how important it is for us to complete this Money Cleanse program together.

This is why I've created a Money Cleanse success agreement for you to read through and sign. It's a promise to yourself to go all in so that you can experience a stress-free money mindset and get to have and experience everything you truly want. This agreement is a form of accountability to yourself and a reminder of what you've set out to accomplish.

Money Cleanse
SUCCESS AGREEMENT

I take on the challenge of the 30-Day Money Cleanse by committing to the following:

1. **I take full responsibility for my progress and results. I understand that I am the only person who can make myself successful.**

2. **I agree to trust and follow the step-by-step Money Cleanse program.**

3. **I agree to show up fully for myself in this program. This means carving out time in my schedule to read the book and complete the exercises each week.**

4. **I understand that the work will not always be easy.**

However, I will not give up, and I will make my work in the Money Cleanse a priority.

5. **I agree to ask others for help and accountability when I have challenges.**

6. **I understand that successful people stay open to learning and improving. I commit to going through all the program material (even if I am already familiar with some of the concepts) and taking it to a new level of mastery.**

7. **I give myself full permission to go for my biggest dreams.**

Name: ....

Date: ....

All of this wonderful preparation will set you up for success in your Money Cleanse, but success doesn't mean that you will do everything perfectly. You'll be developing new habits and mindsets, and there will be times throughout the Money Cleanse that you will forget, slip up, and regress to your old scarcity ways. If you get triggered into a fixed mindset, remember that this is a money journey and that your skills and habits will evolve over time. It can be tempting to throw in the towel when you make your first "mistake." Remember that these bumps in the road are where the magic happens, and how you react to them can make or break the success of your Money Cleanse.

For example, let's say you set up times in your calendar to focus on your Money Cleanse each week, but something comes up, and you end up late for work and miss your appointment with yourself. It would be easy to think something terrible like *There you go again, messing up! You'll never be successful in your money life.* But these types of hiccups are inevitable, and there are much more powerful ways to deal with them. First, play detective. Why didn't you make the appointment with yourself? If a surprise work meeting was the culprit, why didn't you just reschedule your Money Cleanse meeting for a better time? Was it truly work that got in the way, or was it that you are still avoiding facing your finances?

Whatever the reasons and circumstances, approach them from a place of compassion and understanding. Remember all of those reasons why money is tough? It's no wonder you aren't chomping at the bit to get started. To be honest, you'd almost have to be crazy to *want* to get started!

It will help you to know that it's not possible to "fall behind" in the Money Cleanse. True, there are four weeks assigned to the

Money Cleanse program, but if it turns out that you spend ten days on Week Three or even three weeks on Week Four, you are not behind. Saying that we're behind is another sneaky way of giving ourselves permission to punish ourselves and then eventually throw in the towel. We think, *I'm so behind and delinquent on this, what's the point of even continuing? I've already messed this up so much.* That's not going to work!

It's all happening as it should. Trust the process, continue to move forward despite hiccups and setbacks along the way, and treat yourself with the kindness that you would a friend going through something similar.

Here's a checklist to set yourself up for success as you kick off your 30-Day Money Cleanse:

☐ Create time for the program in your life.

☐ Put it in the calendar for each week.

☐ Sign the success agreement.

☐ Get excited!

CHAPTER FOUR

WEEK ONE
OVERVIEW

> "Instead of looking at the past, I put myself ahead twenty years and try to look at what I need to do now in order to get there then."
>
> —DIANA ROSS

WHAT DO YOU WANT TO accomplish in the next thirty days or over the course of this program? What accomplishment would make you say, "Wow! That Money Cleanse was so worth it!"? It could be one (or many) of your financial goals. For example, you might want to get out of credit card debt, create a rainy-day fund to protect yourself in case of an emergency, go on a vacation you've been dreaming about, or save up for your first home. The goal might even be something more subjective or a feeling that you want to experience in your life, like peace of mind in your financial life, feeling powerful in your financial decisions, or reducing the day-to-day guilt and worry that you feel when it comes to your money.

If you have a first gut instinct, go with it. We tend to muddle things the more we mull them over. Also, your intended accomplishment can and likely will change a bit throughout your Money Cleanse, so don't put a tremendous amount of pressure on yourself to choose the perfect intention. You'll have chances to adjust!

Dream big when you set your intention. Why? One of the craziest and coolest things about intentions is that they usually happen. It might sound too good to be true, but this phenomenon actually has foundations in neuroscience. When you set an intention, you are directing the reticular activating system (RAS) in your brain toward this desired outcome. The RAS functions in images and works on closing the gap between what we envision and our present situation. It reconciles what we want with where we are. The RAS is the part of our brain that filters out all of the sensory information that we don't need. The best part is that because it works in images, the RAS can't tell the difference between an image and real life.[19]

Setting our intention for the Money Cleanse puts this process in motion. Our RAS gets to work on achieving what we want. And it gives whole new meaning to the famous William Arthur Ward quote, "If you can imagine it, you can achieve it."

What do you want to get out of your 30-Day Money Cleanse? Set your intention.

....

....

....

....

....

....

....

....

....

....

The funny thing is that when it comes to our money lives, we often can't even imagine having what we want, because it can feel so far off from where we are. You might believe that having a healthy relationship with money is absolutely impossible, or that saving up to buy your first home is completely out of reach. Here are some strategies to maximize your intention's success.

Start a visualization practice.

Visualization is an incredibly powerful technique to help us achieve our goals and intentions. This has been demonstrated by exercise physiologist Guang Yue from the Cleveland Clinic, who did a study in which he divided participants into two groups. The first group performed physical exercises for twelve weeks, while the other did only "mental contractions" of the same exercises—meaning that they visualized the exercises in their minds—for the same period of time. At the end of the training, the first group had increased the physical strength of the focus area by 53 percent. The group that had only performed mental contractions through visualization also increased the physical strength of the focus area—by 35 percent![20] As you can see, visualizing our intention can have a tremendous impact on our results.

Incorporate a visualization practice of your intention into your day-to-day life. Make sure to use all of your senses. If your intention were already true, how would you feel? Take in the details, including smells, sounds, and feelings to make it even more real.

Tips for Effective Visualization

- Visualize when you are relaxed.
- Visualize using all five senses.
- Practice visualizing by watching yourself living your intention from an outside perspective and by seeing your intention through your own internal perspective.
- Write a detailed script of what you want to visualize.
- Visualize successes only.
- Visualize correcting or recovering from a mistake.
- Visualize what you see, as well as the feelings that the images produce.
- Be creative and have fun!

Create powerful money mantras.

We often think of mantras—things we say to ourselves repeatedly—as positive, but your current money mantras are probably not very inspiring. You might say to yourself, "I'm just terrible at money," or "I'm bad at math, so I'll never be able to take care of my finances." Negative money mantras like this keep you from taking actions and steps toward achieving your goals, and they turn into self-fulfilling prophecies.

Week One

When we say something to ourselves over and over, sooner or later we'll take actions that are consistent with what we tell ourselves. These actions lead to results that reinforce or perpetuate our money mantras. For example, if you tell yourself that you'll never be able to take care of your finances, you'll either take no action at all, or you'll take actions that are consistent with someone who is not able to take care of their finances. When an important decision needs to be made, you might avoid it completely, take advice from a coworker with similar money mantras, or even take a random guess because you think you wouldn't be able to figure it out anyway. Consequently, that decision either isn't handled or isn't handled very well, and you don't get the results that you'd hoped for. This is when you think, *See?! I'm just terrible at dealing with my finances*, and your money mantra is reinforced. It's a vicious cycle!

OLD **MONEY MANTRA**

I'm just bad with money. I never thought this was something I could do.

RESULTS

Inaction. Decisions you aren't happy with. Decreased financial wellness.

NEW **MONEY MANTRA**

I have everything I need to be a savvy investor.

RESULTS

Taking action. Decisions you are happy with. Increased financial wellness.

You've probably used mantras that don't serve you well for years—maybe ten, twenty, or even fifty years—so they aren't going to go away overnight. While you can't remove them from your self-talk vocabulary immediately and permanently, you can replace them with mantras that are powerful and that serve your greater intentions and goals. For example, "I make conscious and intentional financial decisions" or "I have everything I need to deal with my personal finances in a powerful way." Even if you have to fake it until you start to believe it, these powerful money mantras will begin to inform your financial decisions and actions and will move you toward your intentions rather than away from them.

Play devil's advocate to understand why it's actually not impossible.

We can take the money mantra exercise to the next level by completely debunking our existing mantra from the get-go. We do this by finding evidence that it's not true. If your negative money mantra is that you are just hopelessly terrible with money, find some examples where you made positive or beneficial financial choices. If those are hard to come by, it's okay to start with neutral ones!

You can also gather evidence by thinking about why you made certain decisions in the first place. Would anyone else in your position have made the same decisions? Knowing what you know now, you'll most likely make a much more positive and informed decision next time.

When we gather the research and reasons to debunk our negative money mantras, they lose a lot of their power. You might not have a book full of counterevidence, but reasonable doubt is enough evidence for me!

Chat with those who have done it.

When you have a big, amazing intention that feels a bit outlandish or impossible to achieve, there is no better way to make it a possibility than to chat with people who have been there and done it. Not only is it proof that achieving your intention is actually possible, but you can also learn how they got there so you can get there more easily yourself.

Because money is such a taboo topic to discuss, you might not actually know whether anyone in your personal network has achieved what you are setting out to accomplish. If that's the case, telling people about your intention will encourage them to share their own experiences. You can also turn to books, especially biographies of people who have achieved financial success, to see how they were able to do it.

TIP: Will you set aside five minutes of time each morning or evening to do a bit of visualization? Or to reach out to friends who have achieved the financial intentions that you are out to achieve? Schedule time in your calendar to take steps toward maximizing your intention.

But wait, there's more! It's not just your intention that determines your results in the Money Cleanse and the success of your financial goals in general; it's also your motivation to play big. Your intention is not only the goal that you're out to achieve, it's also the bigger **why** behind every action that you are going to take over the next month. When you write out your intention for the Money Cleanse, you want to make sure to dig deep and include this deeper reasoning. Yes, the **what** can be exciting and motivating, but the **why** is really what you're out to achieve. It's your true goal.

For example, if your intention is to pay off your credit card debt, think about why that's important to you. Will you feel a huge sense of relief, save thousands of dollars in interest charges, have more money to put toward things you value, or feel at peace?

Week One

Or let's say your intention is to live with less guilt and stress in your money life. What will that provide you with? Will it create the space for you to finally change careers or start a new business? Maybe it will allow you to have the joyful relationship you've always wanted or even just to have more time to spend doing things that are fun for you.

Find your *why* with the "so that" exercise.[†]

Start by writing your intention from page 45, or what you want to accomplish with the Money Cleanse. The reasons behind your intention are important to include, because they are the juicy parts of your goals. They are the driving force behind what you want to achieve. For example, your intentions might be, "I want to save $10,000, pay off my credit card debt, and buy a condo." Then write your answer to the prompt, "So that..."

Example:

I want...

to be wealthy.

[†] "So that" exercise is adapted from Cindra Kamphoff's *Beyond Grit* (Minneapolis: Wise Ink Creative Publishing, 2017).

So that...

I'll have financial freedom.

I can buy and do the things that are important to me.

I can live a full and meaningful life.

I can share meaningful experiences with my friends and family.

Write your intention followed by six responses to get to the heart of your *why*.

I want...

....

....

So that...

....

....

....

....

....

....

....

....

Week One

CHAPTER FIVE

MONEY JOURNAL AND
EXPENSE LIST

Guidelines for Week One

> **"Done is better than perfect."**
> —ONE OF SHERYL SANDBERG'S FAVORITE MOTTOS

ONE OF THE MOST IMPORTANT things I'm going to have you do during your Money Cleanse is keep a money journal, where you write down or type out everything that you spend and earn, and I mean *everything*. Grab a pack of gum at the local bodega, add it to your money journal. Find a quarter on the street, include it in your money journal. It's like a food log, but for your money!

With all the technology, credit statements, and apps we have for tracking our spending and income, this exercise might sound silly, simple, or even redundant. But when we write down or type out what we spend and earn, we can't help but become conscious of it. We reconnect with where our money is going, and it's magic.

As with any new habit, it's important to make this as easy as possible on yourself when you start out. If you're someone who loves physically writing in a journal, carry one around with you. If you find it easier to keep your money journal in a spreadsheet or in notes on your phone, go ahead. If you have an app that allows you to manually enter your expenses (rather than syncing them up automatically), use it.

TIP: Set a calendar reminder to journal your day!

You are inevitably going to miss some expenses or even forget to keep your money journal sometimes. This process is not about being perfect or having the most accurate money journal possible. It's really about the experience of tracking. Try to remember what you missed, but if you don't, it's no problem. Pick up where you left off.

If you continue to forget to keep your money journal, do some detective work. What can you change to set yourself up for success?

You might test out calendar reminders or create fun rewards for yourself when you keep your money journal. The same principle applies: it's much more important to do it than to do it perfectly.

We've included pages for your first thirty days of journaling in the back of this book, but there's no right or wrong way to keep it. At minimum, write down what you earned or spent and what it was for. For example, $5 spent on coffee and a snack or $100 earned for house-sitting. For the first couple of weeks, keep it simple. Later on, you might decide to break your expenses down into more specific categories. I find it really helpful to do some reflection on each expense. How did you feel before you made the purchase and then how did you feel afterward? Did it feel worth it?

MONEY JOURNAL EXAMPLE

Item	Amount	Experience before I bought / earned it	Experience after I bought / earned it
Lunch	$10	Hungry/bored	Satisfied/guilty

Alongside a money journal, another important step on your money journey is to create a list of your daily, weekly, monthly, annual, and one-time expenses. To help you get started, here's a list of common expenses for you to reference:

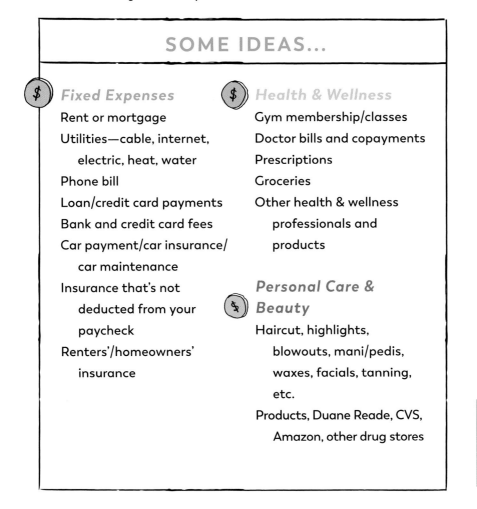

SOME IDEAS...

Fixed Expenses

Rent or mortgage
Utilities—cable, internet,
    electric, heat, water
Phone bill
Loan/credit card payments
Bank and credit card fees
Car payment/car insurance/
    car maintenance
Insurance that's not
    deducted from your
    paycheck
Renters'/homeowners'
    insurance

Health & Wellness

Gym membership/classes
Doctor bills and copayments
Prescriptions
Groceries
Other health & wellness
    professionals and
    products

Personal Care & Beauty

Haircut, highlights,
    blowouts, mani/pedis,
    waxes, facials, tanning,
    etc.
Products, Duane Reade, CVS,
    Amazon, other drug stores

Week One

MORE IDEAS...

Children

Daycare, babysitter, or nanny

Education (current and planning)

Camp and activities

Clothes and toys

Gifts & Celebration

Birthday and holiday gifts

Weddings—gift, shower, hotel, transport, clothes

Donations

Other

Laundry and dry cleaning

Cleaning products

Shopping, tailoring, shoe repair

Professional fees— accountant, taxes, lawyer, coach

Dining out, coffee, drinks

Entertainment—concerts, movies, shows, museums, classes, etc.

Pet expenses

Travel—airfare and airport transport

Transit—taxis, Uber, trains, subway, gas

Subscriptions and memberships—Dropbox, Hulu, Netflix, Spotify, etc.

Jot down anything that applies to your life. This activity might also help jog your memory about other expenses that I haven't mentioned, because my sample list is by no means exhaustive. Take a look at your most recent credit card and bank statements, and go through your calendar to find any expenses that you might have missed.

If you started your list on a very granular level and it's feeling overwhelming, go ahead and lump some of your expenses into broader categories. For example, if you have breakfast takeout, lunch takeout, dinner takeout, weekend dinners, weekend brunches, coffee, and drinks as some of your categories, you might want to lump it all into "dining out." You can always get more specific later on!

Don't worry if you forget to put some of your expenses on this list. Feel free to add to it as you live your life. Reference your money journal for insight. This expense list can and will grow and change. I recommend thinking of it as a living document rather than a finalized list of your expenses.

Where is your money going? List out your expenses.

Expense items

Week One

Expense items

Next, you are going to take the beautiful list you've created and put each expense item into one of three buckets, or categories: (1) needs, (2) frivolous, and (3) not sure.

Needs are items or expenses that are essential to your life, like rent or mortgage, bills, and food. Frivolous spending is anything outside of that. Some items might fall into both categories. For example, you might believe that taking a taxi on the way to work in the morning, rather than walking or taking public transportation, is frivolous, but after a certain time of night, you might view that same taxi expense as a need, due to safety concerns. Similarly, you might believe that your yoga-class membership is a need because it's essential to your health and well-being. On the other hand, you also know that you could do yoga in your living room with online workout videos for a much lower cost. So you might put yoga and taxis into the not-sure bucket or categorize taxis after 10 p.m. as a need and taxis before 10 p.m. as frivolous. It's important to be very specific with your expenses so that it's clear which bucket each one falls into.

EXAMPLE OF BUCKET EXPENSES

TAXIS

NEED	FRIVOLOUS
After 10 p.m.	Before 10 p.m.

GROCERIES

NEED	FRIVOLOUS
Under $75 per week	Over $75 per week

Just because you categorize an item as frivolous doesn't mean that it's bad or that you shouldn't spend your money on it. Frivolous just means that it's not essential or necessary. It might still be a very valuable expense that you get a lot of meaning from (or it might not be).

Go through each item on your expense list and place it into one of the three buckets. For the items that you're feeling unsure of, break them down more specifically to get to the bottom of what aspect of them is frivolous and what aspect is a need. Listen to your gut.

Bucket your spending. What does frivolous spending mean to you? Be specific.

Need/Essential/ Obligation	Not Sure	Frivolous/Luxury/ Nonessential

At this point, you have some incredibly valuable information. You have a list of everything that you spend money on, categorized into three buckets. With this information handy, you can now create the guidelines for the first week of your Money Cleanse.

I'm going to make a couple of recommendations, but what you decide to do in your Money Cleanse is completely up to you. Feel free to accept my recommendations, adapt them in a way that makes sense to you, or reject them completely. I promise, I won't be offended.

Your first challenge is to let go of everything in the frivolous-spending bucket for the next seven days. Remember, it's only seven days!

> **TIP: Spend in cash to reconnect with your spending.**

Your second challenge is to do all your spending in cash for the next seven days. Yes, that includes Amazon, sales sites, and any other online shopping. This is another way to get reconnected with your spending.

Now, spending in cash only isn't for everyone. Some people feel like they actually spend more money when they only use cash, because the cash has already been removed from their bank account, so it feels like they've already spent it. If cash feels more

Week One

like Monopoly money to you, continue to spend as usual (on your credit or debit card).

For most of us, spending in cash makes us feel more conscious of where our money is going, so try it out! It can be a hugely valuable and eye-opening process for your money life.

Again, make this guideline as easy as possible on yourself. Plan ahead for how and when you'll get the cash for your daily life. Will you stop at an ATM once per day or once per week? Will you bring a set amount of cash with you each day or for an evening out with friends? If you prefer not to carry a lot of cash, you can make more trips to the ATM or use a debit card, which feels more like cash than a credit card. Planning is a very important part of the Money Cleanse process.

If you pay your bills via credit card or use a corporate card for work expenses, leave those items as is. Use cash for your day-to-day spending. You don't want the cash guideline to get in the way of paying your bills or handling your finances at work.

The rest is up to you. What guidelines will you live by in Week One of your Money Cleanse? Think back to your intention and stretch yourself. Note that while we've provided ten lines for you to use for your guidelines each week, the amount you set for yourself is up to you! You can start off small.

When you write your guidelines, make sure to write them in

the present tense, as if they are already happening. For example, "I eat breakfast at home three times per week." This might seem like a subtle difference, but it can have a big impact on how we see ourselves living out our first week.

Also, be as specific as possible so that it's really clear whether or not you're sticking to your guidelines. Ambiguous guidelines lead to ambiguous results. For example, if you want to decrease your dining-out expenses, you might write as one of your guidelines, "Dine out less." This is not a specific or helpful guideline, because what does dining out less actually mean? Get specific by listing out how many meals per week you plan to eat out, or how much money you plan to spend on each meal or even for the whole week. You want your guidelines to be crystal clear!

It's also important to incorporate your life into your guidelines. Look through the next week in your calendar and work any plans that you may already have into your guidelines. Remember, the Money Cleanse has to work with your life, but don't be afraid to get creative and push the envelope. If you have dinner plans scheduled with friends this week, what are some ways that you could make those plans fabulously frugal (i.e., more fab for less cost) or fit them into your guidelines? Could you choose a less expensive restaurant, offer to host at your place, or even find a fun, free event

Week One

65

Write your spending guidelines for Week One.

1.

2.

3.

4.

5.

6.

7.

8.

9.

10.

for the group to attend instead? Bring your friends in on this. They might come up with some win-win ideas for your plans together.

Before you head off on your first week of the Money Cleanse, you'll want to create some strategies to set yourself up for success. Hopefully you set some guidelines for your first week of the Money Cleanse that will be a challenge for you and really stretch your current behaviors and habits around money. If that's the case, you might be feeling a bit worried or even cringing a bit. That's a good sign!

Choose your three most challenging guidelines and brainstorm some strategies to make them easier on yourself. What are some situations that might get in the way? How can you prepare for them? How will you reward yourself when you stick to your guidelines?

For example, let's say you decide to bring your lunch to work three times over the next week. Sounds great! What will you do when your best friend at work stops by to ask you to go grab lunch?

Which three guidelines will be most challenging for you? Write down some strategies or ways you can plan in advance to mitigate these challenges.

Example Guideline:	Example Potential Strategies:
I bring my lunch to work three times per week.	• Just say "no" if asked to grab lunch. • Bring lunch four times so I can say yes once. • Go for a walk and enjoy the lunch I brought. • Tell my coworkers about my Money Cleanse.

Guideline:	Potential Strategies:

Guideline:	Potential Strategies:

Guideline:	Potential Strategies:

Brainstorming how you will handle different scenarios that might derail your guidelines can set you up to deal with them powerfully. It's fun to experiment with these strategies. Some will work great and others won't. That's okay! You can adjust and create new and improved strategies. It's all part of the Money Cleanse journey.

Here's your Money Cleanse checklist for Week One:

- ☐ Complete the exercises in chapters four and five.
- ☐ Keep your money journal.
- ☐ Live your Week One guidelines.
- ☐ Test out strategies for your most difficult guidelines.

Week One

WEEK TWO

WEEK TWO
OVERVIEW

> "Too many people spend money they
> earned...to buy things they don't want...
> to impress people that they don't like."
>
> **—WILL ROGERS**

CONGRATULATIONS! GOING FORWARD, we're only going to **add** spending back into our guidelines. Give yourself a pat on the back. It's only going to get easier from here on out.

Before we jump into Week Two of our Money Cleanse, let's check in on our intention. After living your guidelines for the first week, does your intention or goal for the program still feel motivating to you? Is there anything you want to tweak or adjust? Remember, this is the big picture and the goal for reading this book in the first place. It defines what you will get out of this, so make it juicy!

What do you want to get out of your 30-Day Money Cleanse?

Check In with Your Intention

....

....

....

....

....

....

....

....

Next, it's time for a bit of reflection. Each week, we'll go through a reflection exercise on what we've accomplished and experienced during our Money Cleanse. Throughout the last seven days, you've gathered some incredibly important data. By engaging in reflection, you can harness that data and use it to your advantage. This will maximize your Money Cleanse results.

Week One Reflection

What did you miss during Week One, and why?

....

....

....

....

....

....

What didn't you miss during the week, and were you surprised?

....

....

....

....

....

....

What was hard at first but got easier during the week?

....

....

....

....

....

....

Week Two

73

How did it go with filling out your money journal?

....
....
....
....
....

Take a look at your money journal from the week. Does anything stand out to you?

....
....
....
....
....
....

Tally up your total spending. What does it look like compared to previous weeks?

....
....
....
....
....
....

There will always be ways that we can improve. Bring your growth mindset to these reflection questions. If you didn't keep your money journal every day or you aren't feeling like a money master, add the word *yet*. You may not be a money master *yet*, but by the end of this Money Cleanse, you sure will be!

This next exercise is my absolute favorite. When I discovered this mindset shift, it completely blew my mind. It all starts with the things we want. The things we want might be our broader financial goals, like paying down our student loans, building a rainy-day fund, or buying a home, or they might be things we've been daydreaming about or jonesing for, like a weeklong beach vacation or a new laptop.

As always, this is about what gets you excited. There are no right or wrong answers. Don't be afraid to dream big. If you want your own private jet, write it down. If you get joy from simple pleasures like a face mask and a good book, add them to the list.

Week Two

What do you want?

1. Vacation

2. Dinner with friends

3.

4.

5.

6.

7.

8.

9.

10.

Next, why do you want these things? For example, you might want to go on a beach vacation because you're craving some R & R and pampering. Or you might love going to concerts because it helps you unwind and have fun. What are the reasons that you want what you want? What do these items or experiences *actually* provide you with?

What does this provide? What's the value, purpose, or experience?
1. Excitement, exploring, R & R
2. Connection, fun, love, get to unwind
3.
4.
5.
6.
7.
8.
9.
10.

Now here's the mind-blowing mindset shift. When we talk about our goals, we're typically referring to the items and the experiences that we want. We're saving up for the vacation, the new home, to pay down our debt, etc. But the real goal is the purpose or source of our want. Put another way, the goal isn't the **what**, it's the **why**.

In the vacation example, the goal isn't the vacation itself— the goal is to feel relaxed, rejuvenated, and pampered. Going to concerts isn't the goal; it's the fun and excitement that we're after.

77

The vacation and the concert are actually just our current strategies or ways to achieve those experience-based goals. But there are many other strategies or ways to get those goal experiences too.

Let that sink in. Isn't it a relief that you have choices? Yes, you might still choose to go on the beach vacation to achieve your goal of R & R and pampering, but there are many other strategies that will achieve those same goals. You can experience those feelings all the time—even right now, before you've saved up for your vacation. That's such a huge weight off your shoulders! And it's also really exciting!

Why wait another minute to achieve your goals? Enter frugal joys. This is one of my favorite concepts, and I'm excited to share it with you. Frugal joys are free or inexpensive things that make us really happy. They will be different for each of us, because different things make each of us happy, and it will be important (and fun) to test them out. You might get tremendous joy from having a picnic outside on a nice day, and your best friend might love to listen to her favorite podcast. There are countless ways to bring joy into our lives that don't cost a thing (or don't cost a lot). It just takes some brainstorming and planning!

100 Frugal Joys

1. Read a good book.
2. Enjoy a really good cup of coffee.
3. Explore a new neighborhood.
4. Have a picnic.
5. Stop to smell the roses (literally).
6. Find and attend a fun, free event in your area.
7. Listen to a new podcast.
8. Visit a museum.
9. Exercise in a park.
10. Practice yoga at home.
11. Snuggle a pup.
12. Host a brown-bag wine tasting.
13. Meditate.
14. Redecorate using what you already have.
15. Call someone you haven't spoken to in a while.
16. Study a foreign language.
17. Volunteer.
18. Take a free online class.
19. Journal.
20. Read the newspaper or your favorite magazine.
21. Take a bubble bath.
22. Go on a hike.
23. Plant seeds for a future garden.
24. Tackle a fun DIY project.
25. Make your own all-natural beauty products.
26. Give yourself a manicure or pedicure.
27. Take a dog for a walk.
28. Plan a fab frugal date night.

Week Two

29. Go for a bike ride.

30. Bake something delicious.

31. Invite a friend over to chat.

32. Donate clothes to charity.

33. Dream.

34. Host a potluck with friends.

35. Visit an art gallery.

36. Go to the farmers' market.

37. Host a movie night.

38. Indulge in a seasonal activity: apple picking, pumpkin carving, making hot chocolate, looking at fall leaves, etc.

39. Send someone a handwritten note.

40. Send an email to someone you haven't talked to in a while, just to check in.

41. Tour a local business.

42. Stretch.

43. Hang out in a bookstore or library.

44. Grow your own herbs and spices.

45. Watch a play at a local theater.

46. Play a sport.

47. Watch a movie.

48. Go on a run.

49. Listen to live music.

50. Get drinks during happy hour.

51. Tour a winery.

52. Try a new fitness class (the first one is often free!).

53. Play bartender at home.
54. Go to a trivia night.
55. Trade books (or anything) with a friend.
56. Visit relatives.
57. Catch a matinee.
58. Use memberships that you already have.
59. Be a tourist at home.
60. Take a nap.
61. Do absolutely nothing for an hour or two.
62. Watch the sunrise.
63. Watch the sunset.
64. Finish a puzzle.
65. Try a new recipe.
66. Dance.
67. Sing.
68. Make memes.
69. Find a new hobby.
70. Start a blog.
71. Knit.
72. Become an amateur photographer.
73. Draw or color.
74. Juggle.
75. Learn a magic trick.
76. Play an instrument.
77. Watch a documentary.
78. Do calligraphy.
79. Play a board game.
80. Host a game night.
81. Say positive affirmations.
82. Write down one hundred things you're grateful for.
83. Give a hug.
84. Sleep in.
85. Make a playlist of your favorite songs.
86. Go to the beach.
87. Look through old photos.

Week Two

88. Share a story.

89. Make a top-ten list.

90. Look out the window.

91. Rewatch your favorite show.

92. Tell someone you love them.

93. Give a compliment.

94. Do a good deed.

95. Donate five dollars.

96. Rest.

97. Reorganize a room.

98. Take some deep breaths.

99. Spend time in the sunshine.

100. Walk barefoot on the grass or beach.

Now that you know what your true goals are, what are some free or inexpensive ways that you can achieve those experiences or feelings? If your goal is R & R and to feel pampered, what are some frugal ways to achieve that? Maybe you luxuriate in a long bubble bath, sleep in one morning, or enjoy breakfast in bed.

> **What are some strategies to get those experiences that DON'T require money?**

....

....

....

....

....

....

....

As part of your guidelines for Week Two, you will test out three free or inexpensive strategies for achieving your experience-based goals. If you get on a roll, test out more! It's a win-win, because you'll be experiencing more joy without spending more money.

The easier, but less frugal, part comes next. Brainstorm ways to achieve your goal experiences with strategies that do require money. This could include things like your original strategy of a

Week Two

83

beach vacation, spending an afternoon at the spa, or taking a day off work to relax.

What are some strategies to get those experiences that DO require money?

....

....

....

....

....

....

....

You are now armed with an arsenal of strategies to achieve your goals, some that cost money and others that don't. For now, in Week Two of your Money Cleanse, you are only going to incorporate the frugal joys.

TIP: Keep a running list of frugal joys you want to try. Cross them off the list one by one.

Later on, you can pick and choose strategies based on what works best with your happiness allocation. If you're looking to spend less, you can use low-cost or free strategies, and you can also add in some of the strategies that cost money. This means having a lot more of that wonderful goal feeling in your life!

CHAPTER SEVEN:

PUTTING TOGETHER YOUR HAPPINESS ALLOCATION

> **"One step at a time is good walking."**
> **—CHINESE PROVERB**

YOU ARE NOW READY TO face the numbers.

Facing the numbers means quantifying what you spend and earn annually. This might sound like a daunting task, but you've been preparing for this over the last week with your list of expenses and the money journal data that you've gathered.

Why is an annual look so important? When we look at our income and expenses annually, we see the true impact over time of each of our expenses. This way, we have the information to decide how we can spend our money in the most meaningful ways.

For example, you've probably heard this advice before: cut your fancy coffee drink habit, and you'll save hundreds. I heard it too. My daily latte habit cost me $4.30, which didn't seem like a big deal. However, by calculating how much it was costing me on an annual basis ($1,569.50, to be exact), I wasn't so okay with it. I decided that I would much rather put that money toward something else. And that's what I did. I started drinking the free coffee at my office and used the savings to take a trip to Spain with my cousin.

I didn't feel like I was giving something up, because I was gaining something much more important to me. Without looking at the annual numbers, you'd never think that your small cup of joe could make such a big impact. But with this information at the ready, we can make some powerful choices.

> **TIP: Look at each of your expenses on an annual basis to understand the true impact.**

The point of this exercise is not to make you feel guilty or to sway you to let go of your beloved habits. These decisions are up to you! You're just gathering information so that you can make the choices that work best for you. Switching to free office coffee was the right decision for me, but someone else might choose to continue drinking their coffee-shop lattes (and many do!) because that brings them more joy than anything else.

It's also important to look at our expenses annually because some of our expenses don't happen every week or even every month. Trips we have planned, wedding gifts, the holidays, and even haircuts are often forgotten because they don't happen regularly. Still, they can make or break our plan if we forget to include them.

Use your list of expenses along with the information from your money journal to look at each of your expenses annually.

Create Your Happiness Allocation:
OUTFLOWS

Expense Item	How Often?	Current Spend	Annual Spend
Groceries	Weekly	$75	$3,900

....

....

....

....

....

....

....

....

....

....

....

Once you've filled out the chart for each of your expenses, there's some room to experiment. A couple of variables can make a big difference—the cost of the item and the number of times we spend money on the item per year. Let's use a gym class as an example. If I sign up for a class that costs $25 per class, and I take it four days per week, 52 weeks per year, that's $5,200 for one year. Then let's say I test out a less expensive class from another studio that costs $10 per class, but I continue to take it four days per week. That's $2,080 for one year—a savings of $3,120. Or maybe I decide that

Week Two

I really love that first class, so I stick with it for $25 per class, but I only take it once per week instead of four times per week. That class now costs me $1,300 annually (a savings of $3,900).

Playing around with the "how much" and "how often" variables can make a big difference in your annual plan. As strange as it may sound, doing things less often has its benefits. When we go out for lunch every day, it might become routine or even seem like a nuisance, but if we decide to eat out just once per week or even once per month, it feels a lot more special, like a treat. We end up spending less money and deriving more joy from the expense and the experience when we do indulge. Try out some different "how much" and "how often" figures in the following chart. Are there any ways you'd like to reallocate your spending?

Create Your Happiness Allocation:
OUTFLOWS

Expense Item	How Often?	Current Spend	Goal Spend	Annual Spend	Annual Goal Spend
Groceries	Weekly	$75	$65	$3,900	$3,380

Expense Item	How Often?	Current Spend	Goal Spend	Annual Spend	Annual Goal Spend

We will use this information to put together your happiness allocation, which represents what's happening in your money life right now. I call this "getting naked with our finances," but it's not quite as sexy as it sounds. This allocation reflects your inflows (or income) and outflows (or expenses) over the course of a year.

While our income can and will vary at any given point in time, we only have a set amount of money that we get to allocate toward our goals and lifestyle. I call this amount of money our *pie*. Regardless of how much or little we earn, we only get to spend or use each dollar that we have once. We might as well use or spend it on the things that make us the happiest, both in the short- and long-term.

This makes your happiness allocation an extremely liberating plan. You're allocating your money in the way that's going to maximize your joy!

You might think that a plan would be restrictive or make you feel guilty, but it turns out to have the opposite effect. When you don't have a plan, most of your expenses make you feel guilty, because you have no idea if they work with your goals or if you can even afford them. If your happiness allocation includes a certain amount of money each week for things like grabbing drinks with friends or getting manicures, then you get to spend that money guilt-free, because you know that it fits into the plan. It's a beautiful thing!

To put together your happiness allocation, use the golden rule of personal finance:

Create Your Happiness Allocation: The Golden Rule

What do you have available for your goals?

TOTAL INFLOWS - TOTAL OUTFLOWS =
TOTAL AVAILABLE FOR GOALS.

Add up each of your annual expenses and plug that total right into your happiness allocation.

Total Inflows	Total Outflows	Total Available

Then, you just need your annual income. This is usually a lot simpler. If you're a W-2 employee, use your after-tax income (the amount of money that hits your bank account each paycheck) and multiply it by the number of paychecks you get per year. This is usually twenty-four if you are paid twice a month, or twenty-six if you are paid biweekly.

It gets a bit trickier if you are a freelancer or entrepreneur with a variable or less reliable source of income. If that's the case, what can you reasonably expect to earn over the next year? Make sure to factor in taxes; that is money that you won't be keeping, so you can't allocate it to your spending and goals.

Create Your Happiness Allocation:
INFLOWS

Income Item	How Often?	Current Income	Goal Income	Annual Income	Annual Goal Income
Salary	Biweekly	$2,500	$2,750	$65,000	$71,500

Week Two

Add up your annual income, and voilà! You have everything you need to calculate your current happiness allocation.

TOTAL INFLOWS - TOTAL OUTFLOWS =

TOTAL AVAILABLE FOR GOALS

When you first look at this equation, it might not look pretty. And that's okay! You might be spending more than you're making (no wonder your credit card debt is increasing!) or you might not be able to put as much money toward your goals as you'd like. Maybe you don't even know how much you want to be putting toward your goals. All of that is okay.

Before we get to maximizing your happiness allocation and making it work for you, it's important to celebrate this very powerful step of having gathered this information. You laid it all out there, and now you have what you need to do something about it.

Just by looking at your current happiness allocation, you will have some revelations. You might be shocked by how much you spend on Lyft, random things on Amazon, or any number of your own frequent expenses. Sometimes, that simple awareness is all you need to let go of an expense painlessly. Other times, you might decide to keep an expense, but make it less frequent or choose a less expensive option.

It's also possible that, after seeing your current happiness allocation, you feel so overwhelmed by the outcome that you have no idea where to start. Don't stress if you aren't having any life-changing revelations yet. That's okay too.

How to have a financially stress-free holiday season.

There are some expenses in life that we can't plan for; that's why we have a rainy-day fund. But there are also many expenses that we can plan for and just don't. The holidays are a perfect example. They happen every single year. And yet, every year, nearly half of us get stressed out about money around the holidays.[21] The sooner we start planning for them, the less "pain" we'll feel financially. Here's how.

› STEP 1

Get clear on what's important. What are your favorite holiday memories? What made those memories special?

› STEP 2

What do you plan to spend money on this year? (Examples: gifts, travel, parties, dining out, clothes, extra transportation, etc.)

› STEP 3

Add the numbers. And get granular.

What do you plan to spend on this year?	How much will each cost?
5 gifts	$50 each × 5 = $250

› STEP 4

Get fabulously frugal. Is there any way to reduce these numbers while maintaining or increasing their fabulousness?

What do you plan to spend on this year?	How much will each cost?	Can I make it fabulously frugal?
5 gifts	$50 each × 5 = $250	Secret Santa with group: 1 gift for $50

› STEP 5

Make the space for your holiday fund. I highly recommend creating a bucket or a separate account in your online savings accounts specifically for holiday spending (and any of your other larger, less frequent expenses).

› STEP 6

Consider your income. How many paychecks do you have from now until you plan to make each of your holiday purchases?

› STEP 7

Calculate it out. If you plan to spend $500 and you have five paychecks until you plan to spend it, then you'll want to put aside $100 per paycheck.

How much do you want total?	By when (how many paychecks)?	Amount per paycheck
$500	5 paychecks	$100 per paycheck

› STEP 8

Set it up to be automatic. Have whatever amount you calculated per paycheck transfer over automatically to your holiday fund. In the above example, you'd set up $100 to transfer to your holiday fund each time you get a paycheck, so that the cash will be there, ready for you when it's time to make your holiday purchases.

› STEP 9

Plan ahead for next time. Start earlier to minimize your holiday stress next year.

How much do you want total?	By when (how many paychecks)?	Amount per paycheck
$500	25 paychecks	$20 per paycheck

You can apply this exercise to any large expense that you have coming up in the next couple of years to minimize stress and ensure that the money will be waiting for you when you need it. This can apply to your vacations, rainy-day fund, kid's tuition or camp costs, vet bills, and even haircuts.

If you're a freelancer or entrepreneur, it's a great idea to do this with taxes so that you aren't scrambling when your quarterly payments come due. If your income is pretty steady, you can set aside a certain amount per week or month. Or, if you have variable income, you can set aside a percentage of every check.

Week Two

CHAPTER EIGHT

FRUGAL JOYS AND THE LANGUAGE WE USE AROUND MONEY

Guidelines for Week Two

> **"I know for sure that what we dwell on is who we become."**
> **—OPRAH WINFREY**

THE LANGUAGE WE USE AROUND money is really important. Money mantras influence our actions, which create our results, and our results in turn prove or disprove our beliefs about ourselves and money. Utilizing powerful money mantras is a tremendous tool for maximizing our financial success.

Our money mindset is also extremely powerful. When we shift our money goals to be intentional acts of self-love, rather than acts of restriction and self-deprivation, it becomes easy to take the actions that get us closer and closer to our goals.

The journey is in noticing the language, reframing it, and moving forward.

The phrase *can't afford* is a great example, and we hear it all over the place. "I wish I could go on a vacation, but I can't afford it," or "I can't afford to buy that new outfit or piece of furniture." When we use the phrase *can't afford*, it affects our entire demeanor. It's a phrase that comes from that place of scarcity and lack. We are insinuating that we want something but can't have it. We immediately feel deprived.

While there are some things that we truly can't pay for, in many cases, we technically could afford the item or experience that we're talking about by not spending money on other things or by using some form of savings or financing. In most cases, we are actually choosing not to purchase it. *Choosing not to* is a much more powerful phrase, and it's usually true! We are choosing not to take the trip or buy the new piece of furniture because it will take away from another goal or even put us in a financially stressful situation.

When you choose not to do something, it comes from a place of power and abundance—a healthy money mindset. You've weighed your options and chosen the alternative that will bring you more long-term joy and happiness.

TIP: Keep a journal of the common phrases you tell yourself about money. Next to them, write down more powerful replacements.

Other common phrases communicate the idea of having to *cut things out* or *give things up* from your spending plan. You might say, "I have to cut down on my dining expenses," or "I have to give up my gym class." When we cut something out or give something up from our lives, we go back to restrictive mode. It's almost as if the expense is being pried from our hands. It feels like a loss or something that we wanted but don't get to have anymore.

When we *let go* of an expense, on the other hand, it's a completely different experience. The expense is just something extra that we didn't need in the first place, and it falls away. When we reframe our language, our actions follow fairly effortlessly.

I like to use the analogy of an onion. The outer layers of an onion get crunchy and fall away pretty easily. These are expenses that we are ready to let go of. It might be something that we didn't even know we were spending money on, or something that we were just buying out of habit. Whatever the expense is, we're ready

EXPENSE ONION

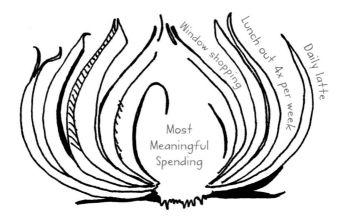

Window shopping

Lunch out 4x per week

Daily latte

Most
Meaningful
Spending

to let it go, so it happens pretty painlessly. It becomes easy to take a different route to work and pass on purchasing a morning muffin, or to avoid shopping for a few weeks. It's not something that you have to consciously make yourself do, it's just an easy shift.

The inner layers of our expense onion, on the other hand, are harder or even really difficult to pull away. These are expenses that we are not ready to let go of. As we progress through our money journey, they might eventually get crunchy and fall away easily, but at this point, they're not ready. And that's okay.

While it's important to challenge yourself during your Money Cleanse, it's also important to honor the journey and the process. Over the course of the next few months and even years, your less important expenses will continue to fall away over time, and you'll be left with the expense items that are most important to you. These are the expenses that are most closely aligned with your values.

By now, you're probably insanely curious to find out which expenses you're ready to let go of and which expenses you aren't. I have just the exercise for you!

In the first column of the following table, you're going to list out expense items that you'd like to test out. Take a look at your money journal and happiness allocation for some ideas. Go wild—you can test out as many expenses as you want.

Then, you're going to write down what value the expense represents to you and the feeling that it achieves. I'll return to my latte example here. Getting that warm latte each morning on my way to work felt like an act of self-love, because it provided me with some comfort.

Next, brainstorm some other ways that you can experience that value or feeling. To experience comfort, I could make coffee at work but use a special mug that I love or keep slippers and a cozy blanket at my desk. If any of those ideas were to work as a sufficient (or even better) replacement for my daily latte, how much would I save? I'd save an extra $4.30 per day, which adds up to $1,570 per year that I could allocate toward something else.

Fill out the chart for each expense item that you want to test. Then, take a look at the result. Is this an expense that you are ready to let go of? If you're not quite sure, use this week of the Money Cleanse to try out the alternatives and see if they give you the value and feeling you're after. If they work, great! If they fall short, you can come up with other ideas or other expense items to test out.

Item	Value It Represents	Feeling or Goal It Achieves	Alternatives?	Decrease in Spend	Decrease in Annual Spend
Latte	Love	Comfort	Special mug, slippers, or blanket at desk	$4.30/day	$1,570/year

Week Two

You are now ready to write your guidelines for the next week of the Money Cleanse. How will your spending look for the next seven days? Make sure to include:

- Your original guidelines for Week One. Adjust any as you see fit.
- Three frugal joys (free or inexpensive strategies that will help you reach your experience-based goals).
- Alternative strategies for the layers of your expense onion that you are ready to let go of.

Write your guidelines in the present tense, continue to keep your money journal, spend in cash only (if that's a strategy that works well for you), commit to no online shopping, and the rest is up to you!

As you write your guidelines, think through the coming week (or better yet, take a look at your calendar) and create guidelines that will work with your existing plans. If you're going away for the weekend, how will you incorporate that into your Money Cleanse? Will you choose fabulously frugal activities, take public transportation to and from the airport, or focus your spending on aspects of the trip that are most important? Talk through it with your travel buddies or a best friend. Planning in advance makes all the difference.

Write your spending guidelines for Week Two.

1.

2.

3.

4.

5.

6.

7.

8.

9.

10.

Week Two

Set yourself up for success by anticipating situations that may come up and derail your Money Cleanse guidelines. How will you handle them? How will you celebrate or reward yourself when you stick to your guidelines? How will you deal with "mistakes" in your Money Cleanse?

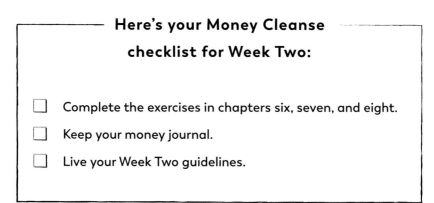

Here's your Money Cleanse checklist for Week Two:

- ☐ Complete the exercises in chapters six, seven, and eight.
- ☐ Keep your money journal.
- ☐ Live your Week Two guidelines.

CHAPTER NINE:
WEEK THREE
OVERVIEW

> **"We can tell our values by looking
> at our checkbook stubs."**
> **—GLORIA STEINEM**

IN WEEK THREE, WE WILL put our money where our heart is and align our spending with our values. It's an action-packed week of goodies, but before we dive in, I want to address the elephant in the room. It's much easier to start something than it is to finish it. At this point in the Money Cleanse, you might be (or you're almost definitely) feeling behind. Or you might be punishing yourself for not participating fully. If you aren't experiencing this yet, take note and come back to this part when you need it.

At some point, we all fall off the Money Cleanse wagon. And

it's actually a great sign! The point where you want to give up and throw in the towel is where the most powerful new habits are built and the biggest progress is made.

First and foremost, forgive yourself for wherever you are in your Money Cleanse. We are a work in progress, and we know that our behaviors, skills, and habits around money can evolve and grow.

Then, reconnect with your **why**. Why did you commit to doing this in the first place? Along the way (and especially after the excitement of a new beginning has worn off), it's easy to lose sight of your motivation or the reason why this is so important to you, but reminding yourself of your **why** can be a game changer for reinstating that motivation.

Here are some ways to incorporate your **why** *into your everyday life:*

 Print it out and tape it somewhere in your office or around your desk.

 Make it your background or screensaver on your phone or computer.

 Read it to yourself in the morning when you wake up or at night when you go to sleep.

($) Have it pop up as part of your alarm clock each morning on your phone.

($) Incorporate it into your daily meditation practice.

($) Share it with your family and friends.

Now all that's left to do is to get back in the saddle and continue on with your Money Cleanse. The key to results? Taking action.

I know you're with me!

Let's reflect on all of the work you did over the past week of your Money Cleanse.

Week Two Reflection

Did you test out your experience-based guidelines? Did they bring you joy?

....

....

....

....

....

....

....

....

How did it go with your happiness allocation? What did you take away from the exercise?

....

....

....

....

....

....

Did you decide to let go of any spending items? How much will that save you per year?

....

....

....

....

....

....

....

Did you miss the items you let go of this week? Why?

....

....

....

....

....

....

....

....

Overall, how did this week of the Money Cleanse go?

....

....

....

....

....

Did you go all in on your Money Cleanse and commit fully? How can you improve for next week?

....

....

....

....

....

....

....

....

Week Three

117

While we tend to focus on what we're not doing right or the mistakes we make along the way, it's much more important to focus on and celebrate our successes. Sadly, we're usually pretty terrible at celebrating our success. We set goals and either hit them and move right along to the next one or miss them and focus on the failure. It's important (and so fun) to celebrate how far we've come and what we've accomplished. As you go through your Money Cleanse, don't forget to track your progress and celebrate.

- How has your spending looked these past two weeks compared to before the Money Cleanse?
- Are you feeling less stressed or more confident about your personal finances?
- Did you get through all of the action items?

How will you celebrate how far you've come? Maybe you'll celebrate with friends, give yourself the afternoon off, or even do a little happy dance all by yourself. Whatever you do, make sure to acknowledge yourself. Given all that you've accomplished so far, just imagine what's possible for the rest of your Money Cleanse and in the months and years to come.

TIP: Write down your money successes each week. How will you celebrate each milestone?

Now let's put your money where your heart is!

CHAPTER TEN:

PUT YOUR MONEY WHERE
YOuR HEART IS

Values-Based Spending

> **"The little things? The little moments?**
> **They aren't little."**
> **—JON KABAT-ZINN**

IT MIGHT SOUND LIKE A no-brainer, but when we spend our time and money on the things that are most important to us, we feel more fulfilled and experience more joy. It makes so much sense and sounds so simple. So why are so few of us actually doing this?

Over time, we tend to accumulate expenses. You might still be getting charged for a subscription that you previously used and loved but no longer care about. Or maybe you got in the habit of doing something each day or once a week and don't even realize that it's not adding any value to your life. Often, expenses pile up because we aren't conscious of what we're spending our money on or aren't in the habit of planning in advance. Maybe we spend money on some things because our friends do and it just seems normal.

Whatever the reason, you most likely have some expenses that aren't aligned with what you really value. To find those expenses, we'll start by identifying what's most important to you.

What makes your life meaningful? I find it helpful to imagine myself looking back on my life when I'm old and gray and picturing what would make me think, *I lived a great life. I did well.* If I had the ultimate perspective on what's important to me, what would it be?

To help you answer this question, you're going to create a values statement, which is a statement that is essential to you and what you are all about. I know—it's big stuff. This values statement will serve as a road map for your life. You can use it to make any decision in your life, including, of course, your financial decisions. It's an extremely powerful exercise!

Read through the list of words on the next few pages.‡ Circle any

‡ Adapted from Steve Pavlina's list of values: https://www.stevepavlina.com/blog/2004/11/list-of-values/.

Week Three

that resonate with you. Go with your first gut instinct, and try not to choose words that you think you *should* choose. Which words or concepts are truly most important to you?

Abundance	Altruism	Belonging	Cheerfulness
Acceptance	Ambition	Benevolence	Clarity
Accessibility	Amusement	Bliss	Cleanliness
Accomplish-ment	Anticipation	Boldness	Clear-mindedness
	Appreciation	Bravery	
Accuracy	Approachability	Brilliance	Cleverness
Achievement	Articulateness	Buoyancy	Closeness
Acknowledgment	Assertiveness	Calmness	Comfort
Activeness	Assurance	Camaraderie	Commitment
Adaptability	Attentiveness	Candor	Compassion
Adoration	Attractiveness	Capability	Completion
Adroitness	Audacity	Care	Composure
Adventure	Availability	Carefulness	Concentration
Affection	Awareness	Certainty	Confidence
Affluence	Awe	Challenge	Conformity
Aggressiveness	Balance	Charity	Congruency
Agility	Beauty	Charm	Connection
Alertness	Being the best	Chastity	Consciousness

Consistency	Delight	Ecstasy	Extravagance
Contentment	Dependability	Education	Extroversion
Continuity	Depth	Effectiveness	Exuberance
Contribution	Desire	Efficiency	Fairness
Control	Devotion	Elation	Faith
Conviction	Devoutness	Elegance	Fame
Conviviality	Dexterity	Empathy	Family
Coolness	Dignity	Encouragement	Fascination
Cooperation	Diligence	Endurance	Fearlessness
Cordiality	Direction	Energy	Ferocity
Correctness	Directness	Enjoyment	Fidelity
Courage	Discipline	Entertainment	Fierceness
Courtesy	Discovery	Enthusiasm	Financial
Craftiness	Discretion	Excellence	independence
Creativity	Diversity	Excitement	Firmness
Credibility	Dominance	Exhilaration	Fitness
Cunning	Dreaming	Expectancy	Flexibility
Curiosity	Drive	Expediency	Flow
Daring	Duty	Experience	Fluency
Decisiveness	Dynamism	Expertise	Focus
Decorum	Eagerness	Exploration	Fortitude
Deference	Economy	Expressiveness	Frankness

123

Freedom	Hopefulness	Investing	Mindfulness
Friendliness	Hospitality	Joy	Modesty
Frugality	Humility	Judiciousness	Motivation
Fun	Humor	Justice	Mysteriousness
Gallantry	Imagination	Keenness	Neatness
Generosity	Impact	Kindness	Nerve
Gentility	Impartiality	Knowledge	Obedience
Giving	Independence	Leadership	Open-
Grace	Industry	Learning	mindedness
Gratitude	Ingenuity	Liberation	Openness
Gregariousness	Inquisitiveness	Liberty	Optimism
Growth	Insightfulness	Liveliness	Order
Guidance	Inspiration	Logic	Organization
Happiness	Integrity	Longevity	Originality
Harmony	Intellect	Love	Outdoors
Health	Intelligence	Loyalty	Outlandishness
Heart	Intensity	Majesty	Outrageousness
Helpfulness	Intimacy	Making a differ-	Passion
Heroism	Intrepidness	ence	Peace
Holiness	Introversion	Maturity	Perceptiveness
Honesty	Intuitiveness	Mellowness	Perfection
Honor	Inventiveness	Meticulousness	Perkiness

Perseverance	Prudence	Sacredness	Skillfulness
Persistence	Punctuality	Sacrifice	Solidarity
Persuasiveness	Purity	Sagacity	Solitude
Philanthropy	Realism	Saintliness	Soundness
Piety	Reason	Sanguinity	Speed
Playfulness	Reasonableness	Satisfaction	Spirit
Pleasantness	Recognition	Security	Spirituality
Pleasure	Recreation	Self-control	Spontaneity
Poise	Refinement	Selflessness	Spunk
Polish	Reflection	Self-reliance	Stability
Popularity	Relaxation	Sensitivity	Stealth
Potency	Reliability	Sensuality	Stillness
Power	Religiousness	Serenity	Strength
Practicality	Resilience	Service	Structure
Pragmatism	Resolution	Sexuality	Success
Precision	Resolve	Sharing	Support
Preparedness	Resourcefulness	Shrewdness	Supremacy
Presence	Respect	Significance	Surprise
Privacy	Rest	Silence	Sympathy
Proactivity	Restraint	Silliness	Synergy
Professionalism	Reverence	Simplicity	Teamwork
Prosperity	Richness	Sincerity	Temperance

Week Three

125

Thankfulness	Trustworthiness	Victory	Willingness
Thoroughness	Truth	Vigor	Winning
Thoughtfulness	Understanding	Virtue	Wisdom
Thrift	Unflappability	Vision	Wittiness
Tidiness	Uniqueness	Vitality	Wonder
Timeliness	Unity	Vivacity	Youthfulness
Traditionalism	Usefulness	Warmth	Zeal
Tranquility	Utility	Watchfulness	
Transcendence	Valor	Wealth	
Trust	Variety	Willfulness	

You might have a short list of words, a very long list, or something in between. Great!

Narrow that list down to the five to ten words that are most essentially YOU.

1. ....

2. ....

3. ....

4.

5.

6.

7.

8.

9.

10.

If you have trouble narrowing down your list, think about which words encompass other words or mean something similar to you. For instance, if you circled love and intimacy or learning and growth, do they mean something similar to you or something completely unique? Which words are important but not the *most* important?

With the five to ten words that you've chosen, you are going to create a statement to live by. I know this can feel like a daunting task; creating your ultimate values statement can take some time.

Work to get something down on paper in the next ten minutes. Putting a time limit on it keeps us from going too far down the rabbit hole of stress and writing variations upon variations. (Yes, we're making Parkinson's Law work for us!) The goal today is to get something down that you can continue to fine-tune and edit as you see fit.

TIP: Set a timer for ten minutes when you write your values statement.

Here are a couple of examples to get you started. Notice that the bolded words came from the values list.

Example 1: *I live a life of **integrity** and **service** by contributing my gifts to the world—**love** and **connection** with others.*

Example 2: *I feel **peace** and **significance**. I approach each day from my best spirit, full of **compassion, gratitude, love,** and **generosity,** while prioritizing my family and friends as well as my path of **financial independence** and **growth.***

Our values statement becomes a road map for our lives. It makes every decision, financial or otherwise, simple, because it hones in on what's most important to us as individuals. It will help us decide which of our expenses align with our values.

Look through your happiness allocation and rank each expense in terms of how much it aligns with your values, with 1 being very aligned and 5 being not aligned at all. You will notice that some expenses are extremely aligned and important, while others are far from it.

Expense Item	Rank

When we see what's important and what's not, it's much easier to let go of our unimportant expenses. This exercise is yet another mindset shift that allows us to add more of what we value and want into our lives, making our lifestyle feel even better. It also creates room for painless saving. Yes, please!

Keep this exercise handy when you write your guidelines for Week Three. There might be some other expenses that you're ready to let go of and some more frugal joys that you'd like to try out.

You can utilize your values statement in other ways too. Take a look at your calendar. Just like our spending is often misaligned with our values, so is our time. How we spend our time is also closely linked to how we spend our money, so it's actually a win-win for our Money Cleanse to take a closer look at how we spend our time too. Then we can reallocate our time toward the things that are most important. It's a happiness allocation for your calendar!

CHAPTER ELEVEN:

THE OPPORTUNITY COST OF
OUR SPENDING

Guidelines for Week Three

> **"Every unwanted 'yes' takes you one step further from freedom, well-being, and time with yourself and loved ones."**
>
> **—KRIS CARR**

THE POINT OF MONEY IS to have and experience the things in life that we want. It's nothing more than a tool! Why not treat it that way and look at each expense in terms of the things that make us the happiest? It's such a great way to gain perspective on how we want to use and spend our money.

What are the three items or experiences that make you the

Week Three

happiest? For example, it might be turmeric lattes, growing your net worth, or getting massages. One of my clients is a fashion designer, and buying clothes is her top happiness-producing item.

Next, what do each of these items or experiences that make you the happiest cost (on average)? For example, a dinner with friends might cost $60 with tip. If you have $2,000 in credit card debt, that's the cost of being debt-free.

What are three items that make you the happiest?	What do these items cost?
Dinner with friends; being debt free; vacation	$60 with tip; $2,000 left on credit card; $1,500 for 5 days
1.	1.
2.	2.
3.	3.

If you're feeling stuck about what exactly makes you happy, read through your values statement for inspiration or take a look at your money journal.

Start with the first item on your list. This should be the number-one item that makes you the happiest of all three. Is it something that you could get more of if you had more money to spend? If the answer is yes, then this is your opportunity cost (more on this shortly), but if the answer is no, then move to the second item on your list. For example, if you listed a gym membership, that would be a no, because you wouldn't want another gym membership if you had more money to spend. You already get all of the benefits from having one membership.

The first item on your list that you answer yes to—meaning that it's something that you could get more of if you had more money—is your opportunity cost. *Opportunity cost* is the cost of the alternatives that you must forgo in order to pursue a certain action. We deal with it all day, every day. Every time we make a decision to do or experience one thing, we give up the opportunity to do or experience something else. For example, when we choose to go to one restaurant, we don't get to try the food or experience the ambience at another restaurant. In the same way, when we choose to use or spend our money one way, we don't get to use or spend it

Week Three

133

on something else. It doesn't matter how much or how little money we have. We only get to use it once. The same rule applies.

We can look at each of our expenses in terms of our opportunity cost—our most coveted goal or what we want the most. If what you want the most is to get a $125 massage or to pay down $10,000 in student loans, then each expense that you incur takes you further away from reaching that goal. We often compartmentalize our money, which is just an irrational money mind game. It is all part of the same pool!

This idea is not meant to make you feel guilty or to discourage you from spending money on a certain item so that you can achieve your goal sooner. When you look at every potential expense in relation to what you want the most, it allows you to decide powerfully whether that expense is worth it to you.

How do we do this? Let's return to our examples. If what you want the most is to pay down your student loans, then you'd look at each of your annual expenses in terms of how much debt you'd be able to pay off. If you were able to pay off $250 in debt instead of spending $250 at the movie theater, would that entertainment expense still be worth it to you?

If you're most excited about massages, letting go of the $250 entertainment expense could pay for two massages. Would that be worth it to you? The best part is, it might be! It's up to you to decide what truly feels like a treat in any given situation.

> **TIP:** This week, look at each of your expenses in terms of your personal opportunity cost.

This is your Money Cleanse challenge for this week: look at every expense you make in terms of your personal opportunity cost. Is it worth it to you?

Here are some ways to incorporate opportunity cost into your everyday life:

- Add a column to your money journal. What does each expense look like monthly or annually? What's the opportunity cost?
- Try out a few different opportunity costs to see which is the most motivating.
- Print out your latest credit or debit card statement and look at each item in terms of your opportunity cost.
- Take your ten largest expenses and figure out the opportunity cost of each.

($) Share your opportunity cost with three people.

($) Create a separate bank account for your opportunity cost. Every time you decide to let go of an expense, add the amount to this account.

Next, list some items that you think you might want to add back into your spending guidelines this week. These might be things you aren't ready to let go of, items that you've missed throughout your Money Cleanse, or things that you know will bring you lots of joy. Then include the average cost of the item, the annual cost, and the opportunity cost. For example, maybe you've been bringing your lunch to work, but you've really been missing your favorite takeout lunch. It costs $10 per lunch and you'd like to have it once per week, which would cost $520 per year. If your opportunity cost is travel, then the opportunity cost of your weekly lunch might be a flight to somewhere cool as well as a night or two in a hotel or an Airbnb.

List some items you want to add back into your spending	What does it cost each time?	What is the annual cost?	What is the opportunity cost?
Daily latte	$4.30	$1570	5-day vacation

After completing this exercise, are there any expenses that you want to add back into your guidelines this week, given the opportunity cost? If so, great! You can add them back in.

One thing that we can do to decrease the opportunity cost of each of these expenses is make them fabulously frugal, meaning more fab while minimizing the cost. Now that you know what's important to you, making something fabulously frugal is simple. It will just take some creativity.

Before you decide whether or not to add each of these expenses back into your guidelines for Week Three, think about how you can make them fabulously frugal. Honor what you miss and let go of the rest. This can decrease the opportunity cost substantially!

——— Make anything fabulously frugal. ———

› STEP 1

Choose an item or activity. Let's continue with the lunch example.

› STEP 2

Pinpoint what you love about it. What do you miss about eating lunch out during the week? Is it getting away from your desk, going for a walk, bonding with coworkers, or enjoying the variety of food?

....

....

....

....

....

› STEP 3

Pinpoint what you don't love. What about grabbing lunch don't you miss? It might be the food itself, the $10 expense, or having to decide what you want.

....

....

....

....

....

› STEP 4

Fab frugal it. When you pinpoint what about getting takeout lunch is most important to you, you can honor what's important and let go of the rest. If you miss bonding with your coworkers or even going for a walk, you could join them for the walk over and then come back and eat the lunch you brought. If you miss

Week Three

variety, you could plan more creative options for the lunches that you bring next week. These are ways that you can experience what you love and miss about something while decreasing the cost. It's fabulous and frugal!

....
....
....
....
....

› STEP 5

Brainstorm with friends. Bring your friends and family in on this so you can come up with ideas together. More ideas mean more possibilities. They might have different reasons why they love your traditions, so you'll want to make sure that your new strategies are a win-win for them too.

....
....
....
....
....
....
....

How will your spending look for the next seven days? Make sure to include:

- Your original guidelines for Week Two. Adjust any as you see fit.
- Ways you will stay connected to your **why.**
- How you will celebrate and reward yourself along the way.
- Any expenses that you are now ready to let go of (new crunchy layers of the onion).
- Any expenses that you'd now like to add back in, based on your values statement and opportunity cost.
- How you will make your expenses fabulously frugal.
- More frugal joys.

As always, look ahead to the next week and incorporate your plans into your guidelines. Share what you are doing with friends. Their support, encouragement, and ideas can make all the difference as you go through your Money Cleanse, and oftentimes, you'll inspire them to look at their spending in whole new ways too.

Week Three

Write your spending guidelines for Week Three.

1.

2.

3.

4.

5.

6.

7.

8.

9.

10.

Here's your Money Cleanse
checklist for Week Three:

- ☐ Complete the exercises in chapters nine, ten, and eleven.
- ☐ Keep your money journal.
- ☐ Live your Week Three guidelines.

CHAPTER TWELVE

WEEK FOUR
OVERVIEW

> **"What makes most people just dreamers versus those who live the dream is that dreamers have never figured out the price of their dreams."**
>
> **—TONY ROBBINS**

YOUR SPENDING IS PROBABLY FEELING pretty great by now. You are spending your money on the things that are most valuable to you, deciding powerfully which expenses are *truly* treats, and filling your life with frugal joys. That's something to celebrate!

Let's kick off this week's Money Cleanse with some reflection.

Week Three Reflection

Did you use your values statement as a road map for any money decisions?

....
....
....
....
....

What can you do to keep your values statement at the top of your mind?

....
....
....
....
....

Did you use your opportunity cost to make any financial decisions this week?

....
....
....
....
....

If you added back any values-based guidelines, how did they feel?

....

....

....

....

....

If you let go of any expenses that weren't adding value, did you miss them? How did it feel?

....

....

....

....

....

Tally up your total spending from the past week. How does it compare with Weeks One and Two?

....

....

....

....

....

....

Week Four

In Week Four of our Money Cleanse, we get clear on what we want and then set up the systems and support networks we need to get there as quickly and easily as possible.

We'll start with our goals. You know all those things you've always wanted to do, have, and experience? You should do, have, and experience them!

We're often too scared to express our goals, even to ourselves. We might think vaguely about what we want, but we don't put a price on our goals and actually let ourselves dream. Maybe we're too worried about how to get there or we're afraid to fail. Let all of that go. Right now, we're going to focus on the goal itself, not the path to getting there. Let yourself dream big!

TIP: Set a timer for ten minutes and let yourself dream about what you want.

Do you want to create a rainy-day cushion, pay down your credit card debt, spend within your means, start investing, or purchase your first home? Do you want to create a financial plan for peace of mind?

What are your top three goals?

Goal 1:

Goal 2:

Goal 3:

How we write our goals is really important. If our goals are vague or out of our control, then we're not setting ourselves up for success in achieving them. The SMART goals method is one of the most widely used and effective methods for goal setting. It states that all goals should be specific, measurable, attainable, relevant, and time-bound.

Now that we know what we want, we can turn our goals into SMART goals.

S PECIFIC—What exactly do you want to achieve? This is the who, what, where, and why of your goal.

M EASURABLE—What exactly will you have, hear, or feel when you achieve your goal? How will you know when you've accomplished it?

A TTAINABLE—Is it possible for you to achieve this goal? Is the outcome in your control? Is it realistic?

R ELEVANT—Is it worthwhile? Are you willing to put in the effort needed to achieve this goal?

T IME-BOUND—By when will you achieve your goal?

When our goals are SMART, we can achieve them more efficiently and easily. We want our goals to be specific and measurable so that we'll know if we've actually achieved them. This also helps us quantify them more accurately. If your goal is simply "Save more money" or "Earn more money," then, technically, all you need to do is save or earn an additional dollar, or even just one more cent. Is that the outcome you're looking for? Probably not.

We also want our goals to be attainable. Is the result within our control? For example, "My husband will stop spending so much money" is not a truly achievable goal, because we don't have direct control over what another person does, as much as we may wish we did! Attainable also means realistic. Based on the information you've gathered about your spending, and on your happiness allocation, is it realistic for you to achieve this goal by the time you plan to? If not, how can you adjust?

A goal's relevance is also extremely important. There are some goals that you might be *able* to achieve, but do you really *want* to? Is your goal a worthwhile and motivating endeavor for you? Without this relevance, we might be going after the wrong things, and we'll feel neither excited to achieve the goal nor fulfilled once we do.

Finally, we want our goal to be time-bound so that we're clear about when we plan to achieve it. Achieving a goal in one year versus ten or twenty years can make a very big difference, so setting a timeline holds us accountable for what we want to achieve.

Here are a couple of example goals: (1) "I want to save more money"; (2) "I want to earn more money."

SPECIFIC—What is "more"? (1) and (2): $10,000.

MEASURABLE—Is this over the next year, five years, or ten years? (1) and (2): Per year.

ATTAINABLE—This will depend on many factors! (1): How does your happiness allocation look? (2): Do you have room to negotiate your salary in your current role? Are you taking on side projects for income?

RELEVANT—Is it worthwhile? (1) and (2): Why do you want to save and earn an extra $10,000 per year? What will it provide you with? Is this motivating to you? How will you feel once you've achieved it?

TIME-BOUND—By when will you achieve these goals? (1) and (2): By the end of the calendar year.

Create SMART goals to maximize success.

Goal Example	
Describe the goal: $4,000 family vacation to Morocco in May	**By when and how will you achieve it?** In the next 18 months by saving $225 per month
Is it measurable? Yes	**Is it relevant?** Yes
Is it achievable? Yes	**How committed are you (1–10)?** 9

Goal #1	
Describe the goal:	**By when and how will you achieve it?**
Is it measurable?	**Is it relevant?**
Is it achievable?	**How committed are you (1–10)?**

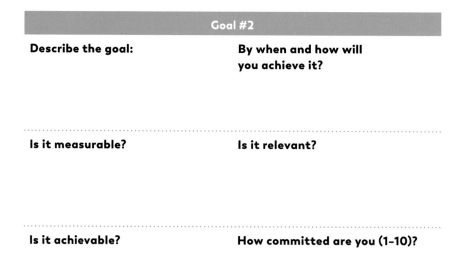

Goal #2	
Describe the goal:	**By when and how will you achieve it?**
Is it measurable?	**Is it relevant?**
Is it achievable?	**How committed are you (1–10)?**

Goal #3	
Describe the goal:	**By when and how will you achieve it?**
Is it measurable?	**Is it relevant?**
Is it achievable?	**How committed are you (1–10)?**

Once you've turned your biggest goals into SMART goals, they become the motivation for everything that you do in your money life! They will inspire you long after the Money Cleanse ends and will keep you excited to maintain your new, powerful money lifestyle far into the future.

CHAPTER THIRTEEN:

CREATE YOUR
DREAM TEAM

> **"Friendship...is born at the moment when one man says to another: 'What! You too? I thought that no one but myself...'"**
>
> **—C. S. LEWIS**

MONEY CAN BE DIFFICULT TO talk about, even with our closest friends and family. For this reason, and many others, we often don't share our money goals. We keep them to ourselves.

This might not seem like a big deal, but if the people we spend the most time with—the people who love us the most—don't know what we are out to accomplish, then they can't support us in those goals. Keeping our goals to ourselves is lonely and can make us feel like we're doing this all on our own. It doesn't have to be that way!

If family and friends aren't aware of our plans, they might even encourage us to do things that are in exact opposition to our goals.

Here's an example. If you were trying to eat healthy and lose weight and didn't tell your best friend, she might unknowingly taunt you with ice cream or pressure you to try her freshly baked dessert because "You deserve it" and "It's so delicious!" She has the best of intentions—she only wants you to be happy. But if she knew that you were on a health kick and understood why you wanted to lose weight, she'd probably be much more supportive of your new, healthy habits.

The same goes for your money! If your best friend knows that you're saving up to buy your first home and, for you, that means a lot less shopping, then she's not going to call you up to hit a sale at your favorite store or encourage you to buy that sweater because "It's just so cute on you." Or, if saving for a home means spending less money on going out, she'll probably be less likely to egg you on to get that next round of drinks.

Think about the people you spend the most time with, near and far. It can be time spent in person, on the phone, over text messages, or even through social media and online chatting. It can be your partner, family members, best friends, colleagues, or anyone who cares about your happiness and well-being but also

Week Four

tends to influence your everyday spending decisions. This is your Dream Team.

Who is on your Dream Team?

....

....

....

....

....

....

....

....

....

....

Now that you know who's on your Dream Team, it's important to tell them! Who wouldn't be honored to be part of your innermost circle of influential friends and family? In order to enroll people in your Dream Team, you'll share your goal(s) or what you've set out to accomplish in your money life. Then, you'll share how they can support you in reaching that goal and, together, you'll develop a plan to make it happen.

Let me share a personal example with you. My husband, Justin, is an extremely important member of my Dream Team. He cares about me, and we make a lot of financial decisions together. He also has a lot of influence over my everyday spending choices. Before we were married, or even engaged, one of my goals was to save up to invest in my business, The Fiscal Femme. I realized that one of the ways that he could help me achieve this goal more quickly and easily was to decrease our everyday food spend. We'd often alternate ordering in and, while that was convenient, the cost really added up!

When I shared my goal with him, we came up with a plan together. He was happy to continue ordering in when it was his turn for dinner, because he loved the variety and convenience. When it was my turn, we'd make something from groceries. Luckily, Justin didn't mind eating eggs and grilled cheese on a regular basis.

As you see, it's really important to include your Dream Team in the planning process, because what they want and value should be taken into consideration too. Together, you can come up with creative, win-win strategies.

Your **why** is a really important factor to share too, especially if the support of your Dream Team means a significant lifestyle change. If you groan to your friend that you *have* to start saving money, it's a lot less likely that you'll get him on board your Dream

Team than if you share with him how relieved and free you will feel after you're debt-free, or whatever your **why** may be.

Let's say you have a friend on your Dream Team who is a big foodie. You currently go out to eat together every week at a nice restaurant that errs on the pricier side. The new plan could be that you go out to eat every other week and try to find foodie places with entrées under twenty dollars. Or you go out for a nice dinner once a month instead of every week.

With each member of your Dream Team, share what you want and why you want it. Then, make a plan together that will help you achieve that goal more quickly and painlessly. If you've been wondering how your new spending habits will affect those you love, worry no more. You can get creative and make your plans fabulously frugal. Just because you're saving more for your goals doesn't mean that you have to skip out on all the fun or give up spending time on things that you value.

> TIP: Commit to sharing one of your financial goals with five people in the next week.

Also, when you let your Dream Team in on your goals, a beautiful thing often happens. They might share their goals with you so that you can support them in whatever they're out to accomplish. It's another win-win.

DREAM TEAM MEMBER #1

What do you want?	Why do you want it?	Make a plan.
Decrease food spend	Save for business investment	I cook dinner when it's my turn; you order takeout when it's your turn

DREAM TEAM MEMBER #2

What do you want?	Why do you want it?	Make a plan.

DREAM TEAM MEMBER #3

What do you want?	Why do you want it?	Make a plan.

What if having conversations about money with your Dream Team absolutely terrifies you? Here are some strategies to kick off the conversation:

- Start small. Share something that you want or one of your goals.
- Ask about their financial goals.
- Tell them that you're reading *The 30-Day Money Cleanse*, to give them some context for where you're coming from (or even blame me for making you do this!).
- Have them brainstorm something fabulously frugal or a frugal joy with you.

💲 Start with the easiest person on your list. Having these conversations gets easier and easier with practice. As you see that people are excited, and often relieved, you'll gain more confidence.

💲 Keep it light. This doesn't have to be a big, scary, daunting conversation. It can be a casual talk over dinner, a glass of wine, or even via text. You'll probably end up kicking yourself for not doing this sooner!

After you complete this exercise, you'll have a plan for your Dream Team, which will be a huge source of support and will make your new money habits so much easier to keep. If you come up with some creative solutions, then your new habits shouldn't impede on anyone's happiness or lifestyle at all—and, best of all, you get to reach your goals.

Week Four

CHAPTER FOURTEEN

MITIGATE ENVIRONMENTAL TOXINS

Guidelines for Week Four

> **"We need to remember what's important in life: friends, waffles, work. Or waffles, friends, work. Doesn't matter, but work is third."**
> **—LESLIE KNOPE, *PARKS AND RECREATION***

NEXT, WE TACKLE OUR ENVIRONMENT, which is another very important and influential factor in our money lives. Unfortunately, it can often be quite toxic!

Environmental toxins are the people, places, and things that get the best of our spending. This could be a friend you hang out with and always come home wondering how you spent so much money, or the store you can't leave without dropping one hundred dollars.

We often think of impulse buys or toxic spending as large, expensive items, but they don't have to be. Anything that we didn't intend to spend money on that we regret later is toxic. And it's not just that single expense that's the problem. Toxic spending can derail our spending for the rest of the day or even for weeks going forward. That's where the real damage happens.

The first step to mitigating environmental toxins is to notice them. When your spending gets derailed, who's there? Are there any people, locales, experiences, or types of items that are frequently involved in your toxic spending? To figure this out, we're going to make a list of your environmental toxins and then come up with plans to deal with them powerfully.

Let's start with people, since they often have the greatest influence on our lives, and we might worry about how our Money Cleanse and new money habits will affect our relationship with them, positively or negatively.

You've already defined your Dream Team, but that still leaves everyone else. How do you deal with the people who aren't your family, your partner, or your close friends? First, think about some typical scenarios where your environment gets the best of your spending. Notice who's there with you.

What are some typical scenarios where your environment gets the best of your spending?	Who's there?
Drink with friend that turns into expensive drinks + dinner	Betsy

In this example, my spending gets the best of me when I go out for a drink with friends and then it turns into multiple expensive drinks and dinner. When I think back on the last few situations where this happened, I notice that my friend Betsy was usually there. Looks like Betsy might be an environmental toxin.

Now, that might sound a bit harsh. Just because someone can be toxic to our spending doesn't mean that they're a bad person or that we can't see them anymore. It's just important to take note and set up some strategies to mitigate the negative effects that these situations have on our spending.

Once we know what our environmental toxins are, we can mitigate them.

First, it's helpful to plan out an allocation or spending goal for each area that your toxic spending shows up. Let's say you and your friend go out for drinks on a regular basis. Based on the first three weeks of the Money Cleanse, you might decide to spend $50 per week on drinks. Let's say $20 of that $50 is typically spent with someone on your Dream Team. That leaves $30 per week for drinks with other people. Alternatively, you could go out for drinks every other week and spend $60 with people outside of your Dream Team. In this way, our spending is very much like pieces of a puzzle. We can test out numbers in our happiness allocation to see if they work.

Here are some strategies to implement once you're clear on your spending goals:

$ If you have room in your happiness allocation and choose to spend your money in this area after considering the opportunity cost—done! You can spend a certain amount of money in this area.

$ If you don't have extra money to spend in this area or you choose not to spend in this area, you can just say no or suggest an alternative that is less expensive or more fulfilling.

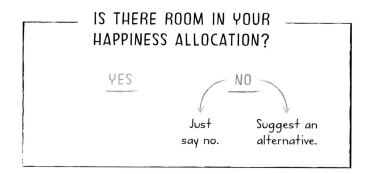

IS THERE ROOM IN YOUR
HAPPINESS ALLOCATION?

YES   NO

Just   Suggest an
say no.   alternative.

We often feel powerless when it comes to how we spend our money with other people in social situations, but we get to choose exactly how we want to handle it.

From here, we can take those toxic scenarios and write down what our spending plan is for each one. If it's shopping, how much do you want to spend on shopping each week or month? Then, for each of these scenarios, what strategy do you think will work best for you and your values? Is it saying yes but staying within a spending goal, just saying no, or suggesting an alternative idea?

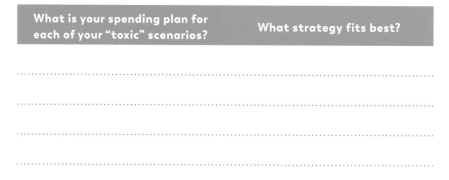

What is your spending plan for each of your "toxic" scenarios?	What strategy fits best?

As you think through your day-to-day routine, you might find some other strategies that work well for you. Add them here and incorporate them into your environmental toxins work. Brainstorm with your Dream Team and take note of what works and what doesn't.

Are there any other strategies that resonate with you?

....

....

....

....

....

....

....

....

....

The guidelines that you've created for how to spend money with members of your Dream Team and how to spend money with everyone else will become another layer of your Money Cleanse guidelines for this week.

Week Four

Group Activities

Group activities are a common trouble spot or environmental toxin. The total cost can often feel out of our control, and it usually ends up costing a lot more than we anticipate. As with anything else, make sure to include group events in your happiness allocation. I recommend adding a buffer of 10 to 20 percent to what you expect the activity to cost. I call this the group tax! It's much better to overestimate in advance than to stress over it and miss out on the joy of the event itself. If it doesn't fit into your happiness allocation, you can say no. Or you can decide to only do one group activity per month and prioritize activities with your closest friends first. It's all about priorities and planning so that you can make the best decisions possible for you.

Let's move on to toxic places and things. We all have those places. Those places where, regardless of what we tell ourselves or intend to do, it's going to be trouble. It could be a favorite store with all those things you don't really need; it could be a certain restaurant where you can't resist ordering the tasting menu; or it could even be your bed, where you shop online late at night!

A trigger place for me is Sephora, or really any beauty counter after I get my makeup done. I end up buying many of the products they use on my face. In the moment, it feels like a great idea, but then later, I feel guilty and realize that I didn't need a lot (or most!) of it.

What are some of your toxic places? If a bunch come to mind, then what are your top three? You can always add to this list as you encounter new ones.

What about toxic things? These can be a bit tricky, because unlike specific places and people, they can turn up anywhere. One of my toxic things is smoothies on the go when I'm running between meetings.

What are your spending trigger places?

....

....

....

....

....

....

....

....

Week Four

What are your spending trigger items?

....

....

....

....

....

....

....

Now, what do we do about this? The easiest strategy for any of these places and things is to just avoid them! It sounds easy enough, but in many cases, there are situations where we can't avoid them. Take the grocery store as an example. It's a trigger place for many people. You might go in with a plan but end up buying a bunch of snacks, toiletries, or other items that you don't need or didn't intend to buy. It can end up costing a lot more than you'd planned, and you might not even walk out with enough food for the week! You can avoid going to the grocery store by buying groceries online, sending your partner, or dining out every meal, but you might find that those strategies don't work with your lifestyle.

In cases where you can't avoid your trigger place or thing, what's your plan? Let's continue with the grocery store example. You know that the grocery store is a trigger place, because you always spend double what you planned and end up with a bunch of stuff you don't need. **What's the plan?** You decide that, based on your average cost for a week's worth of groceries, you're not going to spend more than $70 per week at the grocery store.

It's important to create a reward system for when you stick to your plans. It might sound silly and frivolous to reward yourself, but you'd be surprised by how well rewards really work. Try it out and see! **What's the reward?** If you stick to the plan, you get to buy a little treat for yourself, watch one of your favorite TV shows guilt-free, or do some other small thing that excites you.

Week Four

> **TIP:** Make a list of five potential rewards that you think would be motivating to you. Try them out and see if they work!

Going back to my Sephora example, I could create a guideline to avoid going to Sephora by deciding that if I need to replace a product, I'll do it online. Or, if I do get my makeup done there, I'll only spend $50 to $60, to pay for the service. What's my reward? If I stick to the plan, I can sign up to get my makeup done for the next event I have in six months. Just like with your goals, your spending guidelines need to be very specific so that you'll know if you are sticking with them.

173

SPENDING TRIGGER PLACE #1

If unavoidable, what's your plan?	How will you reward yourself?
Sephora: Only spend $50 to pay for the service.	I can sign up to get my makeup done for my next event.

SPENDING TRIGGER PLACE #2

If unavoidable, what's your plan?	How will you reward yourself?

SPENDING TRIGGER PLACE #3

If unavoidable, what's your plan?	How will you reward yourself?

SPENDING TRIGGER ITEM #1

If unavoidable, what's your plan?	How will you reward yourself?
Takeout: Limit to once every two weeks.	If I do this for three months, I'll buy myself the new running shoes I've been eyeing.

SPENDING TRIGGER ITEM #2

If unavoidable, what's your plan?	How will you reward yourself?

SPENDING TRIGGER ITEM #3

If unavoidable, what's your plan?	How will you reward yourself?

Week Four

——— **How to stop the spending cycle.** ———

Environmental toxins can put us in a tailspin, because they can trigger what I call *the spending cycle*. The spending cycle is the high we get after a purchase, quickly followed by feelings of guilt and shame. The guilt and shame cause us to spend even more to make ourselves feel better, perpetuating the cycle!

This is similar to what can happen with restrictive diets. When we're on a strict diet but slip up and have a piece of cake, we can feel so guilty and terrible for breaking our diet that we end up eating the entire cake. The piece of cake isn't really the problem—it's eating the entire cake that is. This is how environmental toxins work. Our spending can get all out of whack for days, weeks, and even months to come.

If you find yourself caught up in the spending cycle, it can be helpful to have a half-day or even a full-day spending fast. You could also go back to your original guidelines from the first week of the Money Cleanse to break the cycle and get back on track.

The Forty-Eight-Hour Rule

I highly recommend setting a threshold for your spending and instituting the forty-eight-hour rule for anything above that threshold. For example, I won't buy anything that's more than $100 until I've thought about it for forty-eight hours. I find this helpful because once I'm out of the moment, it often won't even be worth the time and effort to go back and buy that thing I *really* needed a day or two before. You can make your threshold $100 or $200 or even $25—whatever makes sense for you.

I've found that the forty-eight-hour rule also works well with couples, when the threshold represents the dollar amount at which you agree to confer with your partner before spending money on something. Anything above $100 or $200 and the two of you will discuss it before spending (unless it's something routine like rent or bills). Having these conversations before-hand can save you from unpleasant surprises and a tremen-dous amount of stress.

Week Four

Knowing that environmental toxins exist is half the battle. And now you have strategies for dealing with them, which you will incorporate into your guidelines for the coming week.

Despite all of your wonderful planning, you're going to come across some roadblocks. Sometimes even the best-made plans don't work. If your plan to handle an environmental toxin doesn't work, don't punish yourself. Use it as a learning experience. What worked and what didn't? Make adjustments to your plan for the future. Over time, your plans will get better and better!

You are now ready to write your guidelines for Week Four of the Money Cleanse. Make sure to include:

- Your original guidelines for Week Three. Adjust any as you see fit.
- Reminders of your most coveted goals (and the motivation for your Money Cleanse) in your everyday life.
- Strategies and plans for people on your Dream Team. (Remember, they are a very important part of the planning process!)

💲 Guidelines to mitigate environmental toxins in your life (people, places, and things).

💲 Rewards for when you stick to your plans for mitigating environmental toxins.

As always, look ahead to the next week and incorporate this week's plans into your guidelines.

Write your spending guidelines for Week Four.

1.
....

....

2.
....

....

3.
....

....

4.
....

....

5.
....

....

6.
....

....

Week Four

7.

8.

9.

10.

Here's your Money Cleanse
checklist for Week Four:

☐ Complete the exercises in chapters twelve, thirteen, and fourteen.

☐ Keep your money journal.

☐ Live your Week Four guidelines.

WELCOME TO YOUR NEW MONEY LIFESTYLE

CHAPTER FIFTEEN

WRAP-UP

Your New Money Lifestyle

> **"The philosophy of lifestyle design is actually quite simple. It suggests that there are limitless ways to arrange and configure your life and that the logistics of living are much more flexible than most of us can imagine."**
>
> **—CLAY COLLINS**

BY NOW, YOUR NEW MONEY habits are no longer guidelines; they have become a lifestyle. After you've completed the Money Cleanse, your relationship with money and your money mindset will be transformed forever. Transformation is like riding a bike. You never forget. If your new money habits ever feel a bit wobbly, know that you can get right back to your detoxed money mindset by revisiting the exercises and principles in this book.

Let's reflect on the past seven days of your Money Cleanse.

Week Four Reflection

What is your highest priority money goal? When and how will you achieve it?

....

....

....

....

....

....

....

Who's on your Dream Team? What plans did you make with members of your Dream Team?

....

....

....

....

....

....

....

....

What strategies or rewards did you use to powerfully mitigate toxic people, places, and things? How well did they work?

....

....

....

....

....

....

....

....

Tally up your total spending from the last week. By now, you should have four weeks of spending!

....

....

....

....

....

....

....

....

....

Before you head off into the world post-Money Cleanse, I want to arm you with a few more key practices and principles. The first is how to allocate your money toward your most coveted goals—a.k.a. how to save money!

The way that we typically view saving money doesn't work. We earn money, live our lives, and plan to use any money that's left over for our savings accounts. The thing is, when we do it this way, there's never any money left over to save. Remember Parkinson's Law? Our expenses will always take up as much as space as we leave available for them.

It's pretty ironic that we prioritize our bills and our everyday expenses over paying ourselves and the things that we want most. Earn money and pay everyone else first? No thank you—that ends now!

When we pay ourselves first, we officially become savers. It's no longer a matter of "Savings would be nice to have" or "I wish it would happen"; we put savings into existence. First we have to shift to the mindset that makes us view savings just like we would any other expense, and then we make it happen.

Make savings happen by answering the following questions:

Where will the savings go? Example: Online savings account

....

....

....

....

....

How much do you plan to save? Example: $100

....

....

....

....

....

How often do you plan to save it? Example: Each paycheck

....

....

....

....

....

....

What actions do you need to take to make it happen?

Example: In order to save $100 every two weeks, I will cook dinner twice per week.

....

....

....

....

....

....

....

The first piece of this equation is where your savings will go. This is actually a really important question. When we have our checking and our savings accounts connected with the same bank, it's often hard to keep money in our savings account. Why? That darn Parkinson's Law again. When we log in, we see money in our savings account and it just feels available to us. Inevitably, we transfer it over to our checking account and use it.

There are people who are able to save money in a savings account tied to their checking account at the same bank, but in my experience, it's not very common.

That's why I highly recommend opening a separate savings

account. The money is still 100 percent there for you when you need it, but it doesn't feel as available to you, because it would take a couple of days to transfer over. Even more importantly, it's out of sight, out of mind. It's a lot easier to save when your checking and savings accounts are separate.

Online Savings Accounts

I'm a huge fan of online savings accounts (also known as high-yield or high-interest savings accounts). These savings accounts are entirely online, and because online banks don't have the expense of running a brick-and-mortar location, they can afford to give us a little more interest. Interest rates are low right now, but you should be able to get around 1 to 1.5 percent annual percentage yield (APY) on your high-interest savings account.[22] That's probably more than one hundred times better than the rate you're getting with your run-of-the-mill bank. Higher rates equals more earning.

Online savings accounts are also usually completely free (so choose a free one!) and have fun features that let you organize your goals into buckets or different accounts. It's a lot more motivating to see specific goals get funded than it is to grow one amorphous savings blob.

You can also set up automatic transfers to specific buckets or goals so that your accounts will grow as planned without having to think twice about it.

These accounts are also separate from your checking account, so the money feels less available for you to spend in your day-to-day life.

Once you have a savings account, your next step is to make saving for your goals automatic. This way, you are officially paying yourself first, rather than waiting to see what's left over.

Because you know how much you need to save for your goals and how much you are saving on a regular basis, you can figure out how long it will take you to reach your goals. Don't let this discourage you. The fact that you are saving money is much more important than how much you're saving. Saving tends to have a snowball effect. Once you get started, you can and will grow from there!

TIP: Set up saving for your goals to be automatic.

If you're living paycheck to paycheck and have no idea how you'll start saving, try an experiment. Set up as little as $5 to transfer to your savings account each week. You'll most likely be surprised by how little you miss that $5, even though you had no idea where it would come from. If this is the case, then double it after a few weeks and see if you don't miss $10. Keep upping the ante every few weeks until you do miss it.

This savings game might seem counterintuitive—especially if you have uncertain income—but just test it out. It's pretty magical!

Next, you'll want to put your money to work. Instead of having all of your savings in one big bucket, you can give each dollar a job by breaking up your savings account into specific goals. You might have a rainy-day fund, a vacation fund, a first home fund, etc. This way it's clear which amounts are dedicated to which goals. It makes allocating money for each goal a lot less confusing and a lot more motivating.

For example, if you're saving $100 every other week, which goal or goals are you funding? Are you funding multiple goals at the same time or choosing to fund your number-one priority goal first before moving on to the next?

How much should you have in your rainy-day fund?

Three months' worth of savings? Two years'? Here's how to calculate how much to set aside for the unexpected.

› STEP 1

First, think through some emergency situations. I know, this sounds like a terribly painful exercise, but it's really helpful to make your rainy-day fund tangible and accurate. For example, plan for scenarios where you lose your job or one of your parents gets sick.

› STEP 2

How many months would make you feel comfortable? If any of the scenarios you listed were to happen, how many months of living expenses would you want to have covered? Three? Six? Twelve?

› STEP 3

What would you spend per month in the case of an emergency? This next step is very important, because your spending would most likely look different if one of these scenarios were to happen. For example, if you lost your job, you would probably spend less in certain areas. What expenses would you let go of? Would you have any additional expenses? From there, you can calculate your total spend per month.

› STEP 4

Calculate your emergency fund. Multiply the number of months by the amount you estimate that you'd spend each month. The total is the amount you'd like to have in your emergency fund.

If this number seems far from reach, that's okay. You can make saving up for your rainy-day fund one of your goals.

─── How to prioritize your goals. ───

Most of us have more than one goal. How many goals do you have, and which goals should you prioritize first?

› STEP 1

First, list out each of your goals.

....

....

....

....

....

....

....

....

....

› STEP 2

Rank each goal in order of priority. Number each of your goals in order of priority, with number one being your highest-priority goal. You can prioritize based on what's most important to you, timing, or necessity. For example, you might decide that having a rainy-day fund to protect yourself in the case of an emergency is more urgent than saving up for your first home, or that you'd rather take a big vacation before saving up for a new car.

› STEP 3

Decide how many goals you want to tackle at once. When we focus on one goal, we achieve it faster, because all of our savings go toward that one goal. Once we've achieved it, we can start working toward the next goal. That being said, it's often difficult to choose which goal gets top priority. When we focus on multiple goals, we make progress on multiple things that are important to us, but the progress on each is shared, so it takes longer to achieve any one goal. Deciding how many goals to tackle at once is a balance. What's most important is that your decision is motivating to you. I recommend choosing one to three goals to prioritize first.

Now you can put your savings toward your top-priority goals. If you have multiple top-priority goals, you can split your savings evenly or allocate more to certain goals than others.

Planning and creating the space for saving makes allocating money toward our goals automatic and simple, and we can also strategize to make the other areas of our money lives as easy and straightforward as possible.

We have a tendency to make our financial lives more difficult than they need to be. We accumulate checking and savings accounts, have 401(k) plans and IRAs in multiple places, and try to remember to pay fifteen different bills on time. Why not make it easy by simplifying, creating systems, and automating wherever possible?

Take inventory and simplify.

List out each of your accounts on the lines below. First, categorize the assets (things you own) as checking, savings, retirement, brokerage, and other accounts.

Then categorize the liabilities (things you owe) as credit card, student loans, mortgage, and other debt. Subtract your total liabilities from your total assets to get your net worth. Note that your net worth has nothing to do with your self-worth. It's just a great number to have on hand so that you can track your wealth as it grows.

....

....

....

....

....

....

....

....

Looking at this list, are there any accounts that you can close or roll over to make your life easier? Does each account have a good justification to earn its place in your money life?

It might not seem like a burden to have three or four retirement accounts, but when you're checking in on what you have in each, it can get pretty tedious. Just remembering all the passwords is a feat in itself!

The life-changing magic of tidying up—your money!

In her book *The Life-Changing Magic of Tidying Up*, Marie Kondo teaches us to declutter our lives by letting go of any items that don't spark joy. Sound familiar? It's very similar to the exercise we did with our expenses. Why have all those extra expenses weighing us down when they don't bring us joy? The connection between decluttering our homes and our money lives doesn't stop there. Decluttering our homes can actually be great for our financial lives as well. First of all, if we're more conscious of what makes it through the front door, we'll definitely start buying fewer things. Not only do things cost money to buy, but they also cost money to maintain, repair, and store. What's more, when we have fewer things, we can be more organized and spend less time rummaging through our stuff in order to find what we're looking for. Another perk is not having to repurchase things that we can't find. Even more, consuming less is also better for the environment. Simplicity and joy—wonderful mantras for every area of our lives!

Once you've simplified your accounts as much as possible, it's time to set up systems and automate. Set up automatic payments wherever you can. If you're worried about not noticing certain expenses, over-drafting accounts, or credit card fraud, set reminders to check your balances and schedule time to look through your statements. Many companies will even send you a statement before the automatic billing goes through. Where else can you automate your financial life?

By now you might be thinking, *This all sounds great, but when will I have the time to do this post-Money Cleanse work?* It's time to have a money party!

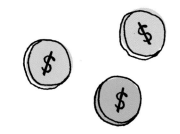

CHAPTER SIXTEEN:

MONEY
PARTIES

> **"Time is a created thing. To say, 'I don't have time,' is to say, 'I don't want to.'"**
> **—LAO TZU**

BEFORE YOUR MONEY CLEANSE, YOU might have dealt with your money pretty haphazardly. We have a tendency to put off whatever is not urgent in our financial lives, and over time, we continue to place it on the back burner. Urgent things might (or might not) get done, but the nonurgent items hang over our heads and stress us out. This could be checking in on your spending, that bank fee you want to negotiate away, or that 401(k) rollover you continue to put off. I have a solution: money parties!

Money parties are time that we set aside to deal with our financial to-dos.

First, you have to create the time. I recommend having money parties every two weeks. Is there a day of the week or time of day that typically works well for you? You can always adjust your schedule as the date gets closer, but I find it really helpful to have a recurring calendar date for a money party every two weeks. Some people love having their money parties on weekend mornings, on an evening after work, or even during work, if it's a quiet time.

TIP: Set up recurring calendar reminders for your money parties.

As with anything else, we get better at having money parties with practice. I recommend allotting more time to your money parties in the beginning, while you get the hang of them. Over time, they'll get easier and faster, so don't give up if your first couple take longer than you'd like.

Who's there at these parties? Invite your partner or family! It's really important to bring them in on the money party fun, even if it's only once per month. We want the people who are part of our financial lives to share in our goals and celebrations. It also makes our lives and relationships a lot less stressful when there's specific time allotted to talking about our finances, rather than having them pop up in conversations (and arguments) all the time.

Plus, reaching our goals is a lot more fun and effective when we include our partners and families.

If you've never talked to your partner about money, you're not alone. Here are some ways to ease into the conversation:

- Start with the fun part—your goals! What do the two of you want? Why is this financial stuff even important?
- Share one money memory you have from growing up.
- Share one of your fears around money.
- Tackle one financial to-do together. (Make it an easy one, so you'll feel accomplished!)

If your partner isn't interested in joining you on your money journey, here are some ideas:

- **Lead by example.** This can take time and feel a bit unfair, but it works! When your partner sees how well things are going for you and that your goals are feasible, they'll be inspired to join the conversation.

- **Share why it's so important to you.** Why are you focusing on your financial well-being?

- **Entice them with things that they want!** That's the whole point of it all anyway.

- **Ask them to test out the Money Cleanse for a trial period.** Instead of trying to commit to a new money lifestyle together right away, let them dip their toes in. How would it be to play along for a week?

You might be wondering what one actually does at a money party. Great question! You get to set the agenda for each party, but I have some suggestions.

A money party is a great time to:

- Check in on your spending and earnings for the period.

- Check in on your progress toward your goals, and reevaluate as needed.

- Celebrate successes and milestones you've achieved along the way.

- Check in on your investments and retirement accounts.

- Have any money conversations that you've been putting off.

($) Simplify your accounts.

($) Negotiate away fees or cancel payments or subscriptions.

($) Set up automatic payments.

($) Revisit the Money Cleanse exercises.

Most importantly, make your money parties fun! I call them *parties* for a reason. You might decide to play some music, get cozy, have your favorite beverage, or set up a fun outing or reward for afterward. Paying attention to your money doesn't have to be boring and tedious. Make it part of date night with your partner or get some friends together for a group money party. After the money party is over, hang out or go out together.

Test out different ways to make your money parties fun. If it's not enjoyable, try out other strategies until it is.

Use this chart to plan out your next money party. Start with whatever is most important. At first, it might make sense to have an A-list and a B-list. The A-list is for things that you will most certainly get done, and the B-list is for things that would be nice to get done. This way, you won't overwhelm yourself with a five-hour money party on your first go. Then, brainstorm how you will make it fun and how you will reward yourself for showing your money some love.

SET UP YOUR FIRST MONEY PARTY!

Time & Day	Agenda	Fun Factor	Reward

CHAPTER SEVENTEEN

ONWARD
AND UPWARD

What's Next in Your Money Journey?

> **"The more you praise and celebrate your life, the more there is in life to celebrate."**
> **—OPRAH WINFREY**

YOU DID IT! CONGRATULATIONS ON completing your Money Cleanse. This calls for a celebration! Before you move on to your next goal or whatever is next in your money journey, it's important to acknowledge how far you've come and celebrate that success.

Did you achieve your intention?

....

....

....

....

....

How much did you save toward your goals over the course of your Money Cleanse?

....

....

....

....

....

....

How do you feel?

....

....

....

....

....

....

....

While it's hard to quantify confidence and peace of mind, you can quantify your savings, and that's such a fun thing to do!

To continue tracking and celebrating your success, use page 228.

Over time, it will be important to revisit all of the exercises you completed during your Money Cleanse. You can reference the following financial bliss checklist, which covers everything we've done, as well as how often you want to check in with the various exercises. This will provide you with everything you need to maintain your new, positive money habits going forward.

Each item comes with a suggested timeline. You can add these to your money party agendas throughout the year. Better yet, go ahead and schedule each checklist item into your money party agendas right now. You can rest assured knowing that you created the time to achieve them.

> **TIP:** Keep this financial bliss checklist in an easy to reference place for future money parties.

FINANCIAL BLISS CHECKLIST

Item	How Often?
❏ Define what frivolous spending currently means for you.	❏ Check in every six months.
❏ Keep a money journal.	❏ For three weeks before and after you put together your happiness allocation (or forever if you like!)
❏ Check in with why you want things. Brainstorm and test other ways to get the same feelings (the true goal).	❏ Regular monthly practice.
❏ Tally your total annual expenses.	❏ Check in or adjust every three months.
❏ Tally your total annual income.	❏ Check in or adjust every three months.
❏ Put your happiness allocation together.	❏ Check in or adjust every three months.
❏ Know your core values.	❏ Check in once a year.
❏ Know the opportunity cost of your spending.	❏ Check in once a year.
❏ Come up with your three most coveted goals.	❏ Check in every three months.

Item	How Often?
❏ SMART your three most coveted goals.	❏ Check in every three months.
❏ Create your Dream Team and make a plan.	❏ Check in every six months.
❏ Create guidelines for everyone else.	❏ Check in every six months.
❏ Create plans for your toxic places and things.	❏ Check in every six months.
❏ Open a high-interest savings account for your most coveted goals.	❏ Check in every three months.
❏ Decide how much to allocate to each goal in your savings account and make it transfer automatically.	❏ Check in every three months.
❏ Schedule biweekly money parties to track your success and progress.	❏ Every two weeks.

This checklist also serves as a great recap of all of the concepts and exercises that you completed over the course of your Money Cleanse. It's a big accomplishment!

Once you've celebrated, you can start thinking about what's next. There is always more to learn, and there are always places you can grow in your money life. Just by completing the Money Cleanse, you have made tremendous progress and built some amazing momentum. Let's keep it going. What will you do next? It could be another book, a course, a specific action or habit— whatever you want!

You might decide to continue to focus on your money mindset. You could choose to grow another area of your financial wellness, whether that means making a plan for paying down your debt, learning to invest, understanding your retirement savings, or increasing your income.

The 30-Day Money Cleanse is an incredible foundation for your financial well-being. Each time you reread this book (and I suggest that you do!), it will be a brand-new adventure, and you'll gain new insights and revelations. It's been an honor and a pleasure to join you in your Money Cleanse journey.

What's next in your money journey?

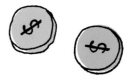

"**If you can't fly, run; if you can't run, walk; if you can't walk, crawl; but by all means keep moving.**"

—MARTIN LUTHER KING JR.

ACKNOWLEDGMENTS

I'M BURSTING WITH GRATITUDE FOR the countless investments made in me in order for this book to come to life. I am blown away by the wisdom, sponsorship, love, encouragement, ideas, introductions, and time that so many gave me. I am forever grateful.

Thank you…

My parents, Kathy and Eric Feinstein, for being the best parents in the world and my forever role models. For my education and for encouraging my growth and curiosity. Mom, for sharing in my dreams and always encouraging me to play full out in my career and personal life. Dad, for teaching me that I can be whatever I want to be and how to go out and get it.

Leigh Eisenman, my incredibly talented agent, for being my unwavering champion, sharing my vision, and guiding me seamlessly and tirelessly throughout each step of this process. I really couldn't have done any of this without you.

Laura Zoltan and Ben Reed, for introducing me to Jesseca Salky, and Jesseca Salky for introducing me to Leigh! It really is the perfect fit.

Meg Gibbons, my brilliant editor at Sourcebooks, and the rest of the amazing Sourcebooks team, for getting and sharing our vision and championing *The 30-Day Money Cleanse.*

My mentors Lauren Smith Brody, Lindsey Pollak, Sallie Krawcheck, and Tiffany Dufu, for showing me how class-act authorship is done.

My work moms and wives Amanda Folk, Belma McCaffrey, Erika Alpern, Jena Booher, Shabari Nayak, and Tina Chopra, for guiding me in my path and putting up with my craziness.

My ladies Ashley Anton, Brittany Topilow, Kristen Hageman, Laura Paliani, and Laura Zoltan, for always listening, inspiring and sharing this journey with me.

Mentors Adria Starkey, Becky Sharon, and Richard Federman, for all the incredible honest advice and coaching throughout the years.

Kristen Veit, for being the unstoppable force behind the Fiscal Femme operations and marketing.

Gemma Leghorn, for editing of my proposal, and Harper Spero, for introducing me to Gemma and for championing me and my work every step of the way.

My lady tribe Alicia Navarro and Jessica Banks, for showing me what's possible and that there's always room for some fun.

My TRIBE Elana Reinholtz, Andrew Fried, Lauren Cecchi, JP Pullos, Jessie Yoh, Elizabeth Eiss, Paige Cecchi, Ben Bechar, and Mollie McGlocklin, for helping me get this book out into the world. Jill Ozovek, for being my constant sounding board and partner, and David Burstein, for your coaching and wisdom leading up to launch day.

Dan Ariely and Jeff Kreisler, for helping me find my money tribe and for making money funny.

My dearest Eli, for giving me a very strict deadline to get my manuscript done and then for inspiring and surprising me every day since you were born with your strength and spirit. You are pure joy!

Michelle, for taking the best care of Eli while I sat in my office and ran around the city working on this book.

Kate, Nathan, Bennett, and Chloe, for being our second family. It really takes a village.

My best friend and sister Ariel Feinstein, who was my willing and supportive guinea pig (she's still not sure why her credit cards are in the freezer).

My in-laws (or in-loves, which is more fitting): Linda and Jim Gerstley, thank you for your boundless support.

Jillian, Kaley, Leah, Heather, Ben, and Meika: I'm so lucky to call you my siblings (and niece!).

My amazing Granny who reads everything I write and loves and supports me even when she thinks I'm crazy!

My Bubbe Shirley, you will forever be my definition of strength and feminism.

For my community and all the incredible people who have shared their money journeys with me (you know who you are!). I am so honored to get to go along for the ride, and I can't thank you enough for what you've taught me.

The love of my life, Justin, for being my number one fan and champion. For your partnership and for giving me the space and time to write a book despite the time and financial constraints of having a newborn. Your relentlessness to find solutions, have-it-all outlook, and way you just enjoy life are an inspiration and lesson for me, always. I'm so blessed to walk through life with you as my partner.

ENDNOTES

1   Experian, "Newlyweds and Credit: Survey Results," (May 2, 2016), https://www.experian.com/blogs/ask-experian/newlyweds-and-credit-survey-results/.

2   Tony Mecia, "Poll: 13 Million Americans Commit Financial Infidelity," CreditCards.com, February 2, 2016, https://www.creditcards.com/credit-card-news/financial-infidelity-poll-secret-account.php.

3   Daniel Kahneman, Alan B. Krueger, David Schkade, Norbert Schwarz, Arthur A. Stone, "Would You Be Happier If You Were Richer? A Focusing Illusion," *Science* 312, no. 5782 (June 2006): 1908–1910, https://doi.org/10.1126/science.1129688.

4   Daniel Kahneman and Angus Deaton, "High Income Improves Evaluation of Life But Not Emotional Well-Being," *Proceedings of the National Academy of Sciences* 38, no. 107 (September 2010): 16489–16493, https://doi.org/10.1073/pnas.1011492107.

5   Dan Ariely, "The Pain of Paying: The Psychology of Money," February 1, 2013, YouTube video, 14:51, posted by Duke University—The Fuqua School of Business, https://youtu.be/PCujWv7Mc8o.

6   "Stress in America: The State of Our Nation," American Psychological Association (November 1, 2017): 2, http://www.apa.org/news/press /releases/stress/2017/state-nation.pdf.

7   "Stress in America: The State of Our Nation," 2.

8   "Report on the Economic Well-Being of U.S. Households in 2016–May 2017," *Report on the Economic Well-Being of U.S. Households*, Board of Governors of the Federal Reserve System, last modified June 14, 2017, https://www.federalreserve.gov/publications/2017-economic-well-being -of-us-households-in-2016-executive-summary.htm.

9   Cameron Huddleston, "69% of Americans Have Less Than $1,000 in Savings," GOBankingRates, September 19, 2016, https://www.go bankingrates.com/saving-money/data-americans-savings/.

10   Monique Morrissey, "The State of American Retirement," Economic Policy Institute, March 3, 2016, https://www.epi.org/publication /retirement-in-america/#charts.

11   Erin El Issa, "NerdWallet's 2017 American Household Credit Card Debt Study," NerdWallet, November 2017, https://www.nerdwallet.com/blog /average-credit-card-debt-household/.

12   Anna Brown and Eileen Patten, "The Narrowing, but Persistent, Gender Gap in Pay," *Fact Tank*, Pew Research Center, April 3, 2017, http://www .pewresearch.org/fact-tank/2017/04/03/gender-pay-gap-facts/.

13   Anne-Marcelle Ngabirano, "'Pink Tax' Forces Women to Pay More

than Men," *USA TODAY*, March 27, 2017, https://www.usatoday.com /story/money/business/2017/03/27/pink-tax-forces-women-pay-more -than-men/99462846/.

14   Scott Hankins, Mark Hoekstra, Paige Marta Skiba, "The Ticket to Easy Street? The Financial Consequences of Winning the Lottery," *Vanderbilt Law and Economics Research Paper No. 10–12* (March 2010): 1–28, http:// dx.doi.org/10.2139/ssrn.1134067.

15   Pablo S. Torre, "How (and Why) Athletes Go Broke," *Sports Illustrated*, March 23, 2009, https://www.si.com/vault/2009/03/23/105789480/how -and-why-athletes-go-broke.

16   George S. Clason, *The Richest Man in Babylon*. (Oxford: Myriad Editions, 2011; New York: Penguin, 1926).

17   Carol S. Dweck, *Mindset: The New Psychology of Success* (New York: Random House, 2006).

18   Carol S. Dweck, "The Power of Believing that You Can Improve," filmed November 2014 in Norrköping, Sweden, TED video, 10:21, https:// www.ted.com/talks/carol_dweck_the_power_of_believing_that_you _can_improve.

19   Tobias van Schneider, "If You Want It, You Might Get It. The Reticular Activating System Explained," Medium, June 22, 2017, https://medium .com/desk-of-van-schneider/if-you-want-it-you-might-get-it-the -reticular-activating-system-explained-761b6ac14e53.

20   Vinoth K. Ranganathan, Vlodek Siemionow, Jing Z. Liu, Vinod Sahgal, Guang H. Yue, "From Mental Power to Muscle Power—Gaining Strength by Using the Mind," *Neuropsychologia* 42, no. 7 (2004): 944–956, https://doi.org/10.1016/j.neuropsychologia.2003.11.018.

21   David Mills, "Big Meals, Tight Schedules and Wallets: What Stresses Us Most at the Holidays," *Healthline*, November 30, 2015, https://www.healthline.com/health-news/what-stresses-us-most-at-the-holidays-113015#2.

22   Spencer Tierney, "Best High-Yield Online Savings Accounts of 2018," NerdWallet, December 19, 2017, https://www.nerdwallet.com/blog/banking/best-high-yield-online-savings-accounts/.

BIBLIOGRAPHY

Ariely, Dan. "The Pain of Paying: The Psychology of Money." YouTube video, 14:51. Posted by Duke University—The Fuqua School of Business, February 1, 2013. https://youtu.be/PCujWv7Mc8o.

Brown, Anna and Eileen Patten. "The Narrowing, but Persistent, Gender Gap in Pay." *Fact Tank*, Pew Research Center, April 3, 2017. http://www.pewresearch.org/fact-tank/2017/04/03/gender-pay-gap-facts/.

Clason, George S. *The Richest Man in Babylon*. Oxford: Myriad Editions, 2011. First published 1926 by Penguin (New York).

Dweck, Carol S. *Mindset: The New Psychology of Success*. New York: Random House, 2006.

Dweck, Carol S. "The Power of Believing that You Can Improve." Filmed November 2014 in Norrköping, Sweden. TED video, 10:21. https://www.ted.com/talks/carol_dweck_the_power_of_believing_that_you_can_improve.

Hankins, Scott, Mark Hoekstra, and Paige Marta Skiba. "The Ticket to Easy Street? The Financial Consequences of Winning the Lottery." *Vanderbilt Law and Economics Research Paper No. 10–12* (March 2010): 1–28. http://dx.doi.org/10.2139/ssrn.1134067.

Huddleston, Cameron. "69% of Americans Have Less Than $1,000 in Savings." GOBankingRates, September 9, 2016. https://www.gobankingrates.com /saving-money/data-americans-savings/.

Issa, Erin El. "NerdWallet's 2017 American Household Credit Card Debt Study." NerdWallet, November 2017. https://www.nerdwallet.com/blog/average -credit-card-debt-household/.

Kahneman, Daniel, Alan B. Krueger, David Schkade, Norbert Schwarz, and Arthur A. Stone. "Would You Be Happier If You Were Richer? A Focusing Illusion." *Science* 312, no. 5782 (June 2006): 1908–1910. https://doi.org/10.1126/science.1129688.

Kahneman, Daniel and Angus Deaton. "High Income Improves Evaluation of Life but Not Emotional Well-Being." *Proceedings of the National Academy of Sciences* 38, no. 107 (September 2010): 16489–16493. https://doi .org/10.1073/pnas.1011492107.

Mecia, Tony. "Poll: 13 Million Americans Commit Financial Infidelity." CreditCards.com, February 2, 2016. https://www.creditcards.com /credit-card-news/financial-infidelity-poll-secret-account.php.

Mills, David. "Big Meals, Tight Schedules and Wallets: What Stresses Us Most at the Holidays." *Healthline*, November 30, 2015. https://www.healthline .com/health-news/what-stresses-us-most-at-the-holidays-113015#2.

Morrissey, Monique. "The State of American Retirement." Economic

Policy Institute, March 3, 2016. https://www.epi.org/publication/retirement-in-america/#charts.

"Newlyweds and Credit: Survey Results." Experian, May 2, 2016. https://www.experian.com/blogs/ask-experian/newlyweds-and-credit-survey-results/.

Ngabirano, Anne-Marcelle. "'Pink Tax' Forces Women to Pay More than Men." *USA Today*, March 27, 2017. https://www.usatoday.com/story/money/business/2017/03/27/pink-tax-forces-women-pay-more-than-men/99462846/.

Ranganathan, Vinoth K., Vlodek Siemionow, Jing Z. Liu, Vinod Sahgal, and Guang H. Yue. "From Mental Power to Muscle Power—Gaining Strength by Using the Mind." *Neuropsychologia* 42, no. 7 (2004): 944–956. https://doi.org/10.1016/j.neuropsychologia.2003.11.018.

"Report on the Economic Well-Being of U.S. Households in 2016–May 2017." Board of Governors of the Federal Reserve System. Last modified June 14, 2017. https://www.federalreserve.gov/publications/2017-economic-well-being-of-us-households-in-2016-executive-summary.htm.

"Stress in America: The State of Our Nation." American Psychological Association (November 1, 2017): 2. http://www.apa.org/news/press/releases/stress/2017/state-nation.pdf.

Tierney, Spencer. "Best High-Yield Online Savings Accounts of 2018." NerdWallet, December 19, 2017. https://www.nerdwallet.com/blog /banking/best-high-yield-online-savings-accounts/.

Torre, Pablo S. "How (and Why) Athletes Go Broke." *Sports Illustrated*, March 23, 2009. https://www.si.com/vault/2009/03/23/105789480 /how-and-why-athletes-go-broke.

van Schneider, Tobias. "If You Want It, You Might Get It. The Reticular Activating System Explained." Medium, June 22, 2017. https://medium.com /desk-of-van-schneider/if-you-want-it-you-might-get-it-the-reticular -activating-system-explained-761b6ac14e53.

ABOUT THE AUTHOR

Ashley Feinstein Gerstley is a certified life coach specializing in personal finance. She earned a degree in finance from the Wharton School at the University of Pennsylvania and has worked in the financial services industry for more than ten years. She founded her company, The Fiscal Femme, in 2012, and dedicates herself to sharing the power and freedom that come from improving one's relationship with money. Ashley has empowered thousands of people in their financial well-being through her corporate wellness programs, one-on-one coaching, online courses, speaking engagements, and frequent contributions to print and online media outlets. As a trusted money expert, she has been featured in *Forbes*, NBC, *Glamour*, and *Business Insider*. She lives in Hoboken with her husband, young son, and dog.

Your money excuses end here. Ashley Feinstein Gerstley lays out a simple yet highly effective strategy for you to overcome your financial hurdles. The workbook style of *The 30 Day Money Cleanse* helps you confront what's standing between you and financial control.

—Erin Lowry, author of *Broke Millennial*

I really enjoyed reading *The-30 Day Money Cleanse*! What I appreciated the most about it is that it's a beautifully simple and holistic guide that incorporates so much behavioral finance. I think this is so important for people to comprehend and incorporate. This book is a must-read for every woman (and man) looking to improve their financial lives. It will make a significant difference in the life of its readers.

—Adria Starkey, president, Finemark National Bank & Trust

Wow! This book is so much more than a financial guide but an experience that every woman NEEDS in getting her life on track! Specifically for those of us focusing on our career: when we are in a strong place financially, we can take more risks in our career and negotiate better salaries. I love so many things about this book but I especially love the freedom it creates. In *The 30-Day Money Cleanse*, Ashley has created a fantastic money resource for women that actually works, helping us tackle our biggest money frustrations and magnify our career success. A must read for anyone who has felt stressed and trapped by funds!

—Lauren McGoodwin, founder and CEO, Career Contessa

Isn't it time you lived your life exactly how you want to? Ashley will show you how in her terrific book, *The 30-Day Money Cleanse*. She gives you all the psychological and financial tools you need to reshape your money mindset and take control of your financial life. I couldn't put it down!

—Barbara Huson, author of *Sacred Success*

Unlike a juice cleanse or the master cleanse, *The 30-Day Money Cleanse* is actually quite delicious. Assuming, like me, you intend to eat all the money you save on this steady diet of financial freedom. Yum, Ashley, yum!

—Jeff Kreisler, bestselling author of *Dollars and Sense* and editor-in-chief of PeopleScience.com.

The 30-Day Money Cleanse offers actionable wisdom so women can reshape their financial lives, ditch the money guilt, and transform their overall well-being in the process. Ashley provides a step-by-step program to help readers make better choices, and makes a typically daunting topic fun and straightforward. Great for anyone looking to think differently about money.

—Laura Vanderkam, author of *What the Most Successful People Do Before Breakfast*

Ashley is one of the essential finance gurus of our generation, and in this book, she offers a powerful new paradigm for thinking about money, budgets, and frankly our happiness. It's essential reading for millennials, and people of all ages would do well to follow her prescriptions.

—David Burstein, author of *Fast Future*

Money is so much more than what's in your wallet. For many of us, it is our self-worth and can be incredibly freeing—or incredibly crushing. Ashley understands that we must first unpack our relationship with money before we can command it. Her money cleanse is accessible and it holds you accountable. This is going to change your life!

—Claire Wasserman, cofounder of Ladies Get Paid

[A] cheery and easy-to-follow guide to creating a healthy personal relationship with money… Gerstley's book offers a solid first step for those just entering the workforce or anyone still in need of developing good financial habits and dealing fearlessly with personal finances."

—*Publishers Weekly*

Money Journal

Date	Amount	Purchase & Notes